This Sporting Laugh

Other books by Norman Giller

The Marathon Kings
The Golden Milers
Olympics Handbook 1980
Olympics Handbook 1984
Olympic Heroes (with Brendan Foster)
The Book of Cricket Lists (with Tom Graveney)
Top Ten Cricket Book (with Tom Graveney)
Cricket Heroes (with Eric Morecambe)
Banks of England (with Gordon Banks)
The Big Fight Quiz Book (Robson Books)
TVIQ Puzzle Book
Lucky the Fox (with Barbara Wright)
Watt's My Name (with Jim Watt)
My Most Memorable Fights (with Henry Cooper)
How to Box (with Henry Cooper)
Henry Cooper's 100 Greatest Boxers
The ABC of Soccer Sense (with Tommy Docherty)
The Rat Race (with Tommy Docherty)
The Book of Rugby Lists (with Gareth Edwards)
The Book of Tennis Lists (with John Newcombe)
The Book of Golf Lists
Fighting for Peace (Barry McGuigan biography, with Peter Batt)
TV Quiz Trivia
Sports Quiz Trivia
Know What I Mean? (with Frank Bruno)
Eye of the Tiger (with Frank Bruno)
Mike Tyson, For Whom the Bell Tolls (with Reg Gutteridge)
Gloria Hunniford's TV Challenge
The World's Greatest Cricket Matches
The World's Greatest Football Matches
A Stolen Life (novel)
Crown of Thorns, The World Heavyweight Championship (with Neil Duncanson)
The Seventies Revisited, with Kevin Keegan

Books in collaboration with Jimmy Greaves

This One's On Me
The Final (novel)
The Ball Game (novel)
The Boss (novel)
The Second Half (novel)
World Cup History Book
GOALS!
Stop the Game, I Want to Get On
The Book of Football Lists
Taking Sides
Sports Quiz Challenge
Sports Quiz Challenge 2
It's A Funny Old Life
Saint & Greavsie's World Cup Special
The Sixties Revisited
Don't Shoot the Manager

This Sporting Laugh

Written and compiled
by **Norman Giller**

Illustrated by David Edwards

Robson Books

Acknowledgements

Author Norman Giller wishes to thank Jeremy Robson and his editorial team, and in particular Editor Louise Dixon and Production consultant Bob Crocker for their encouragement and expertise; also Michael Giller for his Apple-a-day computer skill, artist David Edwards for his graphic support, and, most of all, those many people in the sports world who kindly helped with the compilation of the stories that appear in this book.

This book is dedicated to the memory of ***Harry Miller****, an exceptional football reporter and good pal with whom I enjoyed* This Sporting Laugh.

First published in Great Britain in 1994 by Robson Books Limited
Bolsover House, 5-6 Clipstone Street, London W1P 7EB

British Library Cataloguing in Publication Data
A catalogue record for this book is available
from the British Library

ISBN 0 86051 952 X

Typeset and designed by Norman Giller Enterprises,
Ferndown, Dorset, England
Printed by The Guernsey Press Company Ltd,
Guernsey, Channel Islands

Contents

Introduction

Sport has become too serious a business. There is too often a snarl instead of a smile on the modern face of sport, and too many of today's professionals have forgotten how to enjoy This Sporting Life. But here in *This Sporting Laugh* I intend to prove that sport can, to quote my old pal Jimmy Greaves, be a funny old game.

In a 40-year career earning my daily bread as a sportswriter, I have been lucky to be in a position to collect at first hand scores of sporting anecdotes. I first started putting together a jamboree of amusing sports stories and off-beat quotes for an 'Odd Balls' column on the dear old *Daily Herald* back in the early 1960s. It was a collection I continued during ten years writing for the *Daily Express*, particularly when in harness with the one and only Eric Morecambe on a 'Sports Smile' column. Then, composing a weekly 'Funny Side of Sport' column for the *Sunday Express*, I was able to call on my many friends in the sports world to furnish me with funny stories from their sporting lives. I take this opportunity to thank each and every one of them for putting up with me. The laugh's on them.

For the last eleven years I have been in a privileged position as a scriptwriter for *This Is Your Life*, trusted with the job of putting on paper the life stories of some of our greatest sports idols. This has helped me feather my nest of tales, many of which I pass on in the following pages. I promise to keep a low profile when re-telling the tales that have made me laugh, but there will be occasions when I need to come to the surface to explain how I managed to stumble on previously unpublished stories.

I shall now get out of your way and leave you to chuckle your way through *This Sporting Laugh*. Enjoy!

1: The Great Characters

This is a collection of tall-sounding tales about some of the greatest characters to have stepped on to the sports stage. All the stories are true.

GEORGE BEST once went through an entire match in which, to win a bet, he played the ball only with his left foot. In another game, he passed the ball only to team-mate David Sadler, who was playing in the middle of the Manchester United defence. 'David had moaned at me before the match that I never passed the ball to him,' said George. 'He was sick to death of receiving it by the time the game was over.'

Best was as famous for scoring with girls off the pitch as with his spectacular goals. When asked if it was really true that he had bedded four Miss Worlds, George's stock reply is: 'That's not right. One of them didn't show up.'

A true story that George tells is of the day late in his playing career when he went to a Manchester casino with a former Miss World on his arm. He won more than fifteen thousand pounds at the table before cashing in his chips. It was the wee small hours of the morning when he returned to a swish hotel accompanied by his beautiful girlfriend and with his pockets bulging with ten-pound notes. 'A little Irish nightporter showed us up to our room,' recalled George. 'I slipped him a tenner tip and asked him to bring up a bottle of bubbly.' By the time the porter was knocking on the door with the champagne, the former Miss World had slipped into a negligée and George was sitting alongside her on the bed counting his winnings. The porter put the tray containing the champagne and two glasses on a side table. As he prepared to leave the room, he coughed apologetically and said in a rich Irish accent, 'Excuse me, George, but would you mind if I were to be asking you something?'

'Of course not,' said George. 'What is it?'

'Well, George,' said the porter, 'just where did it all go wrong?'

DAVID GOWER went one better than George Best's efforts at playing the ball only with his left foot. Batting for Leicestershire against Cambridge University, he decided to take runs only when he played the ball on the on-side. He kept the plan to himself, and his startled partner could not understand why he was continually sent back when the ball went to off.

Gower later explained: 'To be honest, I found myself getting very bored out there so I devised this little private game to keep myself alert. The few times I mis-cued to the off-side I just had to surrender the runs. My partner thought I had gone quite mad.'

England officials were convinced Gower had gone off his head when he and John Morris buzzed the pitch in a Tiger Moth during the England innings against Queensland at Carrara during the 1990-91 tour. Gower's only regret is that he did not put the finishing touch to the operation. 'I had wanted to bombard the pitch with water bombs,' he said, 'but it didn't work out.'

As the biplane flew low over the pitch, England batsmen Allan Lamb and Robin Smith looked up in amazement.

Smith reacted by putting his bat to his shoulder and mimed taking rifle shots at the invader, not knowing that it was his team-mate at the controls.

'Biggles' Gower and Morris were each fined £1,000 by the MCC chiefs. They should have given them medals for bringing a smile to the face of sport.

Dr A.J. (TONY) O'REILLY, billionaire boss of Heinz and former pin-up boy of Irish Rugby, has hundreds of playing-days anecdotes. This is one of his favourites: 'I was playing in a match for Leinster when I put my shoulder out. Just a minor dislocation, you know. The physio was summoned and as he put a firm grip on my shoulder and pushed hard I could not help but let out a yell.

'The physio, a local GP, said, "Come on, O'Reilly, I've just delivered a baby and the mother didn't make half as much fuss."

'"Maybe not," I said. "But you weren't trying to push it back in."'

O'Reilly was playing in a match for Ireland against England at Twickenham during which Phil Horrocks-Taylor cleverly dummied past Irish stand-off Mick English to score a try. 'Horrocks went this way,' said O'Reilly, 'Taylor went that way, and poor Mick was left holding the hyphen.'

LESTER PIGGOTT is the king of the one-line put down. He was once approached by trainer Jeremy Tree, who told him: 'I've got to speak to my old school this weekend,

Lester, and tell them all I know about racing. What d'you suggest I say?' Lester appeared to give the question careful thought before replying: 'Tell them you've got the 'flu.'

I had the pleasure of sitting just a horse's length from the Voice of Racing, Peter O'Sullevan, in the days when we were both writing for the *Daily Express*. Peter was one of the few people Lester used to confide in, and they were always talking to each other on the telephone. One day Peter put the 'phone down with a chuckle and said, 'What a character. Lester won the Prix Kergorlay by a nose at Deauville last week and I asked him if he'd been confident he'd got it in a really tight photo-finish. Lester said, "Didn't have a clue. I wasn't looking!"'

Lester was flying in a helicopter with an owner who wore a monogram on his hand-made shirt. 'Why d'you have your initials on your shirt?' Lester asked. 'In case you forget who you are?'

Few punters have ever lost their shirt on Lester.

TOMMY DOCHERTY is acknowledged as the top man in football for wisecracks. When he took over as the manager of Wolves in 1985, he joked: 'I wouldn't say that it's a long time since Wolves won anything, but when I opened the trophy cabinet two Japanese prisoners of war came out.'

It was the Doc who said he once received a death threat from a Manchester United supporter, who telephoned him to say: 'If you pick goalkeeper Paddy Roche again I shall kill myself.' And it was the rascally Docherty who told the Chelsea directors about one of his rivals for the job of manager at Stamford Bridge: 'If you appoint that man, you won't get a coach – you'll get a hearse.'

It was also Tommy who said of an England full-back, 'I've seen milk turn faster.' I always used to tell the Doc that he should have been a stand-up comedian, and he used to shoot back: 'What you're saying is that I'm a comedian as a manager.' But the man who said he'd had more clubs than Jack Nicklaus finally took my advice, and these days is one of the funniest and most in-demand speakers on the after-dinner circuit.

When Tommy and Spurs manager Bill Nicholson were standing in the Wembley tunnel in the nerve-wracking moments before the 1967 FA Cup Final between Chelsea and Tottenham, he ignored the television camera beaming pictures into millions of homes and quietly whispered in Bill's ear: 'Your flies are undone.'

LEE TREVINO realised his caddie in a charity event at Las Vegas was a novice when he drove off from the first tee and asked how far he was from the green. 'About three blocks,' came the reply.

PRINCE ANDREW has caught the golf bug, and I wonder whether he will become as fanatical a player as his great uncle, the Duke of Windsor, who – when the Prince of Wales – was coached by 'The Maestro' Henry Cotton. When I scripted the late, legendary Henry's *This Is Your Life* tribute, he told me: 'The Prince could easily have been a scratch golfer. I recall an incident when an Irish caddie made him shake with laughter during a round that was played at Gleneagles. The Prince was crouching down trying to work out his line for a long putt, and he asked his caddie's advice. "If I were you sir," he said in a thick Irish accent, "I would hit it slightly straight."'

MAX BAER returned to his corner at the end of the first round of a world heavyweight title eliminator against Joe Louis to be told by his second: 'You're doing great. He ain't laid a glove on ya yet.' Baer replied: 'Well, you'd better keep an eye on the referee then, because somebody's knocking the hell out of me.' Baer was knocked out in the fourth round.

It was Baer who once said to Primo Carnera, when they both tumbled to the canvas in a title fight, 'Last one up's a cissy.' He used to say of himself, 'I've got a million-dollar body and a ten-cent brain.'

Before challenging Carnera for the heavyweight crown, playboy Baer was watched in training by New York boxing commissioner Bill Brown. The commissioner could not believe it as Baer clowned with sparring partners and continually blew kisses to the dozens of beautiful girls crowded round the ring. Brown was disgusted as Baer showed off the latest craze for rumba dancing with one of the girls in the ring, and he told the challenger: 'You're a bum.'

Baer burst out laughing, and replied: 'I think ham would be more fitting, but let's see what you think after the fight.'

As he was announced as champion after stopping Carnera in the eleventh round, Baer leaned over the ropes and shouted to Brown: 'Well, what have you gotta say now?'

'You're still a bum,' he replied. He then added after a pause: 'Carnera's an even bigger bum.'

Baer, who toured the theatres as one half of a double act with another former champion of the thirties, 'Slapsie Maxie' Rosenbloom, did not live to see his son, Max Jr, become a hit on television as Jethro Clampett in *The Beverly Hill Billies*. Max Snr suffered a heart attack while shaving at a luxury hotel in Hollywood, where he worked as a film extra.

When he collapsed at the hotel, a bellboy asked if he should call for a house doctor. 'I'd rather see a people doctor,' said Baer. They were his last words. In true spirit, one of boxing's greatest characters left us laughing.

TED DRAKE, a legendary centre-forward with Arsenal and England, was manager of Chelsea when Terry Venables started out on his career. Ted was a lovely man but a little absent-minded. One day he was giving Terry a lift from the ground and as they sat at traffic lights the manager became completely engrossed in talking tactics. The lights changed twice and angry motorists behind them started sounding their horns. 'The lights are green, boss,' said Terry. 'Oh,' said Ted. 'Sorry. I thought *you* were driving!'

It was Drake who first told the classic story that has since been 'borrowed' by a procession of footballers. This is Ted's original version, which he tells in his delightful Hampshire burr:

'It was in the days when I was playing for Southampton, and the maximum wage for footballers was £8 a week in the winter and £6 in the summer. Yes, it was long before the £4,000-a-week players! George Kay, the man who captained West Ham in the first ever Wembley FA Cup Final, was our manager.

'Before each season started you used to have to queue up to negotiate your terms for the following year. Remember that clubs could pay you less than the maximum, so you can imagine how anxious we used to get as we waited to agree our wages.

'On this particular day our full-back Albert Roberts was first in to see the manager. We crowded round him when he came out and asked what he'd got. Albert, a Yorkie from Goldthorpe, said, "Seven pounds ten shillings in t' season, and a fiver a week in t'summer. I'm reet disappointed, but there's nowt I can do about it."

'I was next in and was ready for a verbal battle to try and get the maximum. But I didn't have to say much.

'"Well, young Ted, you've had a great season," Mr Kay said. "There are clubs interested in you, but we've decided we're not letting you go. You'll be pleased to know we're going to pay you the maximum eight and six."

'"Thank you Mr Kay," I said politely and then went out and reported to my team-mates. Our wing-half Stan Woodhouse was the next man in.

'"You had a good season and we're very pleased with you," said the manager. "We will pay you eight pounds in the winter and five pounds in the summer."

Stan, a lovely Warrington lad, said, "'Ee, but Mr Kay, you've just given young Ted eight and six."

'"Ah, but he's a better player than you lad," said Kay, who was also a Lancastrian.

'Stan pondered on this for a moment and then came back with the blinder: "Not in the summer, he's not a better player ..."'

ALAN BALL was leaving Goodison in a hurry to join the England squad for a summer tour during his days as an idol at Everton. He was holding a suitcase in either hand, and was confronted by an Everton supporter.

"Ere, Al pal, gi's yer autograph,' he said in thick Scouse as he held a blank piece of paper under Ballie's nose.

'Can't you see I've got my hands full?' said Ballie, desperate to catch a train.

'Don't worry, pal,' said the fan. 'Just spit on the paper. That'll do me.'

When Alf Ramsey first selected Norman 'Bites Yer Legs' Hunter in an England team to meet Spain in Madrid, Ballie called for hush in the dressing-room. He then put his hands together and said, 'For what they are about to receive ...'

GARETH EDWARDS listened with a straight face as Welsh team coach John Dawes outlined his plan to introduce codewords at a training session before a match against England.

'When you want the left-side flanker to make a break, the codeword should start with a "P",' said Dawes. 'If you want a break on the right side, use a codeword beginning with "S".' He tossed the ball to master scrum-half Edwards, who put it into the scrum and shouted the codeword, 'Psychology'.

Playing for the British Lions against the Springboks on the 1971 tour, Gareth was stamped on by the giant South African forward Frik du Preez. The Cardiff man was at the bottom of a ruck, and the referee penalised him rather than the player raking his studs across his leg. Gareth let fly with a verbal volley and the referee blew his whistle and stopped the game. He summoned Lions skipper Tom Kiernan and complained, 'This player just swore at me, captain.'

Kiernan looked towards Edwards, who threw his arms

wide in a gesture of innocence. 'What me, ref? I wasn't swearing. I was talking in Welsh.'

Irishman Kiernan nodded his head. 'To be sure, that's what he was doing, referee,' he said. 'He is always jabbering away in Welsh. Perhaps, to your ears, it sounds a foul language.'

The referee rather reluctantly accepted Kiernan's explanation. 'In that case I owe the player an apology,' he said.

Kiernan later asked Gareth: 'Did you swear at the ref?'

Edwards shrugged hs shoulders. 'I swear I didn't,' he said, with a distinct twinkle in his eye.

Gareth was once tackled by England three-quarter John Spencer, a famed joker. As they became engulfed in a ruck, Spencer clung to Edwards and chanted in his ear: 'I'm not a pheasant plucker, I'm a pheasant plucker's son; When I'm not plucking pheasant ... ' It was a verse that John had taught Gareth at their last social meeting.

MIKE GATTING was memorably bowled by Shane Warne's first ball in a Test match in England at Old Trafford in the summer of 1993. As Gatting made the long walk back to the pavilion trying to come to terms with the ball having spun at least eighteen inches, he might have pondered on the fact that he should not even have been at the wicket. He had padded up quickly and gone in at number three because Robin Smith, due to go in first wicket down, had 'gone missing'. Smith, nicknamed 'The Judge' by his England team-mates, was in fact detained in the toilet. The delay did not help Smith. He was soon back in the pavilion after also being bemused by Warne's prodigious spin.

Gatting was famed among his team-mates for his enormous appetite and his spreading waistline. Asked during a 1984 Test in India if he wanted Gatting wider at slip, bowler Chris Cowdrey said to skipper David Gower: 'Any wider and he'll burst!'

DAVID STEEL, making his Test debut for England at Lord's in 1975, had never been in the home dressing-room before. When his turn came to go out to bat for the first time in a Test, he took a wrong turning on the way to the Long Room and finished up in the Gents in the basement. Startled members, so to speak, pointed him in the right direction, and he launched his Test career with a 50.

KEITH MILLER, the greatest of all Australian all-rounders and a larger-than-life character, was leading out the New South Wales team at the start of the first morning's play when an alert member did his sums, and said, 'Skip, we've got twelve players.' Miller hardly broke stride as he shouted over his shoulder, 'One of you had better f*** off.'

JIMMY GREAVES will tell you that the English press are pussycats compared to the piranhas who pestered him in Italy. When Jimmy spent nearly five tormented months in Milan in the summertime of his playing career, he was followed everywhere by a posse of photographers and reporters. And I do mean everywhere.

Greavsie was standing doing his business at a urinal in Milan one day when a reporter popped up alongside and asked him a question. Jimmy instinctively turned and hosed the trousers of the Italian hack, who suddenly felt as if he was a real drip. The reporter, according to Greavsie, said something like, 'Whadda did you spray?'

'I was taking the Pisa,' Jimmy later told me with the biting humour that has made him such a television favourite.

Greavsie scored a record 357 First Division goals during his career, but none easier than the one collected for Tottenham against Fulham at Craven Cottage.

Fulham goalkeeper Tony Macedo had been to see the Harlem Globetrotters giving a basketball exhibition a couple of days before the match. As he collected the ball early in the game, he started to give an impersonation of the Globetrotters in what were the running-free days for goalkeepers before the four-step law. He ran round the penalty area bouncing the ball basketball style, and he then mimed in the clowning style of Meadowlark Lemon as if to throw the ball to an opponent.

He switched his aim to Fulham skipper Johnny Haynes, and the ball slipped out of his hand and straight to the feet of unmarked Greaves, who immediately stroked it into the empty net.

As an embarrassed Macedo retrieved the ball, Jimmy shouted: 'You silly basket!' What Haynes shouted is unprintable!

Jimmy came up with a cracking ad-lib when the 1966 World Cup squad took a break at Pinewood Studios to see Sean Connery shooting scenes for the James Bond film *You Only Live Twice.* Alf Ramsey made a short speech at the end of the visit, thanking *Seen* Connery for his hospitality. Greavsie whispered to his best mate Bobby Moore: 'That's the funniest thing I've ever shawn or heard!'

IAN WOOSNAM was having one of his less illustrious rounds early in his professional career. He had spent more time in the woods than David Bellamy, and was struggling to break 80. There was no chance of him making the cut.

As he stood ankle deep in the rough at the 17th, he asked his caddie: 'What do you recommend I take now?' Back came the reply: 'The next train home.'

BOB HOPE was playing in a golf charity match with President Gerald Ford, who was notorious for slicing off the tee and hitting spectators in general and his bodyguards in particular. Asked how the President was doing, Hope cracked: 'He's two bodyguards under par. To get his score we look down the fairway and count the wounded.'

LLOYD MANGRUM, US Open champion in 1946, was penalised two strokes for blowing an insect off his ball during a play-off for the championship in 1950. 'Next time I'll politely ask the damn thing to take off,' he said.

ROBERTO DE VICENZO, Argentinian golf great, said after being disqualified for signing a 65 card as a 66 in the 1968 US Masters: 'What a stupid I am.'

KEVIN KEEGAN passed on this story of wonderful touchline farce during the World Cup qualifying match against Poland at Wembley in October 1973.

'England were being held to a 1-1 draw in a match they had to win to qualify for the finals in West Germany. I was sitting on the substitutes' bench alongside Bobby Moore, who was next to Alf. There were just five minutes to go when Alf suddenly ordered, "Kevin, get stripped." My Liverpool team-mate Ray Clemence helped me pull off my tracksuit bottoms, and was so keen to help me get on the pitch that he dragged my shorts down to my knees. My embarrassment was complete when Alf had to make it clear that he meant Kevin Hector, not me! By the time the other Kevin got on there were less than two minutes left. It was the shortest England debut on record.'

There was not a funny ending to Kevin's story. England were held to a 1-1 draw and were out of the World Cup ... caught with their trousers down.

TOMMY BURNS, former world heavyweight champion, made his professional debut as a substitute for a friend of his who knocked himself out as he tripped over the top rope as he jumped into the ring. He did not even get to hear the bell.

Burns was one of the shrewdest champions in history, both inside and outside the ring. He had a finger in the promotion of most of his fights, and his sharp business brain amazed the British fight fraternity when he made two title defences in London.

At one stage early in his career he was swindled out of his purse, and he swore it would never happen again. He decided to manage himself and used to insist on receiving his money upfront before throwing a punch in anger.

When he fought British champion, Gunner Moir, at the aristocratic National Sporting Club in 1907 he demanded that his £3,000 purse be paid to him in notes in the ring before the first bell. The money was counted out in front of him, and then he handed it over to a 'minder' before getting on with the business of beating Moir.

Before the fight with Moir, Burns had donned a false moustache and glasses and had slipped into one of his challenger's public training sessions to size up his opponent. He was so confident of beating him after this scouting trip that he put £10,000 on himself to win at even money. The canny Canadian won in the tenth round.

Two months later he declined a purse for defending against Geordie Jack Palmer at the Wonderland stadium in London's East End. Instead he chose to take 50 per cent of the gate money. Spectators arriving to buy their tickets on the day of the fight were amazed to find the champion of the world sitting in the box office. He waited until all the tickets had been sold and then put the takings in a bag, locked it up in his dressing-room under the eye of a guard, and then climbed into the ring to knock out Palmer in four rounds.

At the end of his amazing ring career, Burns renounced boxing and became an ordained minister, preaching peace and brotherly love.

ION TIRIAC, the former Romanian Davis Cup star, was famed on the tennis circuit for his strength and daring. The man who helped shape Ilie Nastase into a world-class performer had been a physical training instructor in the army, drove in the Monte Carlo Rally, and once punched a hole in a dressing-room locker door when in a rage following a defeat in Paris. His reputation for being wildly eccentric increased when he calmly ate a wine glass at a post-tournament banquet, a crunching performance that he is always happy to repeat on request. He became known as the player who could win the crunch points. Now a millionaire tennis entrepreneur, Tiriac has been the driving force behind many of the world's top players.

LYNN 'THE LEAP' DAVIES, long jump gold medallist at the 1964 Tokyo Olympics, was runner-up to Mary Rand for a Sports Personality of the Year award, but he was unable to make it to the presentation ceremony at London's Savoy hotel. The chairman of the sponsors announcing the award winners told a celebrity-packed audience: 'Unfortunately Lynn cannot be with us today, but we send her our love and best wishes.'

I was sitting alongside the one-time world middleweight champion Terry Downes, who has never been exactly the quietest of characters. He shouted for all the guests to hear in that unique Yankee-Cockney accent of his: 'And while you're about it, give 'er a kiss from me.'

It was Downes who, when asked whom he would next like to meet following a shock stoppage by Dick Tiger, replied: 'The bastard who matched me with Tiger.'

MICKEY DUFF was the man who matched Downes with Tiger. Mickey is a larger-than-life character who is one of the greatest raconteurs I have come across in nearly 40 years of mixing (and mixing it) in the sports world.

Digging into his bottomless pit of anecdotes, Mickey came up with this classic: 'In my days as a young manager in the 1950s, I took three fighters over to Belfast to box. I had specifically requested that all three be put on early so that we could catch the late-night ferry back to England.

'I was furious when I found that one of the boys was to go on last, and I was just about to give the promoter a piece of my mind when the boxer told me with great confidence, "Don't worry. I'll get the fight over and done with really quickly. We'll catch that ferry."

'True to his word, my boy got it over inside the first thirty seconds. He collapsed as if pole-axed from the first punch thrown by his opponent.

'As I dived anxiously through the ropes to remove his

gumshield while he lay flat out on his back, he gave me a big wink and said, "I told you we wouldn't miss the ferry."'

It is what as known as a ferry story.

HENRY COOPER once proved to a celebrity audience that he had fast reflexes outside as well as inside the ring. In partnership with Peter Lorenzo, the late broadcaster and father of ITV sports presenter Matthew Lorenzo, I organised a testimonial dinner for Sir Alf Ramsey (which was more than the mean Football Association ever did for him).

Harold Wilson, then Prime Minister, was the chief speaker and Henry Cooper was a top table guest at one of London's swishest restaurants.

While the Prime Minister was on his feet paying tribute to Alf and his England heroes of 1966, a brown mouse ran

the length of the top table until caught by the tail by Henry Cooper, whose left hand moved as quickly as when he was throwing his famous 'ammer.

He handed the mouse to the head waiter, with the comment: 'This little feller's trying to get in without a ticket.' Mr Wilson – it was before he became Sir Harold – said later: 'It's the only time that one of my speeches brought the mouse down.'

Henry, a heavyweight hero for all seasons, was defending his European title against Italian Piero Tomasoni in Rome. 'It was the roughest, toughest fight of my life,' he recalled. 'Tomasoni was a crude fighter who didn't care where his punches landed. One right-hander hit me so low that it dented my foul cup protecting the family jewels.

'The crowd went potty when I knocked Tomasoni sparko in the fifth round, and suddenly it started raining food. I have never seen anything like it. The ring was carpeted with piles of oranges, bread, tomatoes and salami. My lovely old manager, Jim "The Bishop" Wicks, said: "They must think you're an 'ungry fighter, 'Enery."'

BOBBY MOORE, the late, lamented captain of England and a footballing genius, had a great sense of humour buried just beneath the surface of his famous 'Mr Cool' exterior. I once saw him have the presence of mind to pick up the whistle and blow it to stop the game after the referee had been pole-axed by a defender's clearance. It was Bobby who told me the following hair-raising tale:

'I was playing for West Ham at Newcastle on a very windy day. When I went to the centre-circle I couldn't help noticing that the referee had a striking head of shiny black hair.

'Newcastle quickly had us under severe pressure and forced a corner. The ref came and took up a position beyond the near post just a couple of yards from me. I looked at him and then gave a double take. He was as bald as a billiard ball.

'I was fighting to keep a straight face, and he knew it. He gave a sheepish smile and said quietly, "It's okay, Bob, my hair's in my pocket. I washed it last night and I don't want it blowing off and getting dirty."

'I resisted the tempation to say, "Keep your hair on, ref."'

RON 'Chopper' HARRIS had one of the most famed and feared tackles in football, and – as a driving captain – was a key man in the Chelsea team that won the FA Cup and European Cup Winners' Cup at the start of the 'seventies. One day Prince Philip was at Stamford Bridge as the VIP

guest of the then Chelsea chairman Brian Mears.
As Harris patrolled in the Chelsea defence, the Prince mischievously asked Brian: 'Why do they call him Chopper?'
Just as the words came out of his mouth, Ron delivered one of his thundering tackles.
'Oh, I see,' said the Prince.

COLIN 'The Brut' SMART will always be remembered by his England Rugby team-mates as the prop forward who brought the sweet smell of success to the Five Nations championship. Colin was conned into sinking a glassful of after-shave in the belief that it was vintage wine during a wild party in Paris to celebrate an England victory over France. Former England skipper Bill Beaumont commented: 'It caused quite a stink at the time.'

BILL BEAUMONT was England skipper the day that Erika Roe made her headline-hitting streak at Twickenham in 1982. 'Hey, Bill,' scrum-half Steve Smith said as Erika bounced across the pitch, 'there's a bird just run on with your bum on her chest.'

PIERRE DANOS, French scrum-half, was knocked out during a violent match against Northern Transvaal in Pretoria in 1958. Two ambulancemen tried to put the protesting Danos on a stretcher. French prop forward Alfred 'L'Rock' Rocques intervened on behalf of the groggy Danos, and flattened one of the stretcher bearers with a mighty right uppercut. They were getting the stretcher ready for the ambulanceman when he jumped to his feet, bowed to Roques, and shouted, 'Vive la France.' Then he and his colleague ran off with their empty stretcher.

DENNIS LILLEE, one of the all-time great Australian fast bowlers, was a fierce competitor, but he always found time for some banter with his favourite umpire, Dickie Bird. Once after Dickie had turned down his loud LBW appeal, Dennis said: 'I think your eyesight's going, Dickie.'

'No,' replied Dickie, 'it's your eyesight that's going. I'm the ice cream seller.'

Towards the end of his career, when he was combining cricket with pantomime appearances, Ian Botham rapped a batsman on the pads and shouted, 'Owzat!'

Dickie Bird responded with a panto-style chant: 'Oh no he isn't!'

GEOFF BOYCOTT could be really talkative in the middle once he had established himself at the wicket. His non-stop chatter during one innings began to irritate veteran umpire Arthur Jepson. A ball rapped Boycs on the pad, and he was convinced it was missing leg stump, but Jepson raised his finger.

Boycs glared at the umpire on his way to the pavilion. Jepson stared back and said, 'Now we'll get a bit of peace. I got rid of my dog for yapping. Now I've got rid of you.'

BRIAN 'Tonker' TAYLOR, former captain of Essex, once reported umpire Cec Pepper – a notorious leg puller – to Lord's 'for continually breaking wind throughout the day's play and enjoying it despite the protests of the players.'

MUHAMMAD ALI, then known as Cassius Clay, was training in London for his first fight with Henry Cooper in 1963 when he became aware of somebody watching him with intense interest. The man would not take his eyes off him, and Clay started to become unsettled by the man's fanatical stare. He was about to shout one of his acid insults at him when it was quietly pointed out that the uninvited guest was the notorious London gangster Ronnie Kray and that it would be unwise to make any insulting comments. Clay absorbed the information and then shouted, 'Hey, man, *you're* the Greatest!'

I worked as a publicist on the midnight fight in Munich when Ali defended his title against British lionheart Richard Dunn. As a ticket-selling gimmick I arranged for the English hypnotist Romark to go to Munich and put Dunn under an hypnotic spell to help his victory bid.

Just a few months earlier, Romark had suffered a stroke that had left his face contorted, with one eye lower than the other. Ali went into fits of laughter at the weigh-in when Romark suddenly confronted him and said with as wide a stare as he could muster: 'You are doomed to defeat tonight. D-o-o-m-e-d.'

Later that afternoon Romark tucked Richard up in bed and told him the story of Cinderella. Once he was asleep, he kept telling him his fists were made of iron.

When the Dunn entourage got to the stadium, they were annoyed to find an American TV crew in their dressing-room. Manager George Biddles ordered them out, and while the cameraman continued to focus on Richard, his trainer and father-in-law Jimmy

Devanney turned off the dressing-room lights.

This back-fired because Richard was now sitting in a darkened dressing-room while high on a wall facing him a TV monitor was showing pictures of Muhammad Ali in his dressing-room telling the American television public just what he intended to do to his challenger.

Dunn put up a brave, beyond-the-call-of-duty performance before being stopped in five rounds by Ali, who by then was past his dazzling peak.

When he returned to the Munich hotel at 3 am, Dunn was met by a posse of British press men who applauded his performance.

Romark, with tears streaming down his face, pushed his way through the reporters and cuddled Dunn. 'I let you down, Richard,' he sobbed. 'I made your fists turn into iron – but I forgot about your chin!'

HOWARD KENDALL provides this story from his days as an exceptional midfield player with Everton: 'I was playing for Everton against West Bromwich Albion in the days when we had two Newtons in our squad – Henry and Keith. In their tactical talk before the match the West Brom players were told to attack Henry Newton on his left side. 'He hasn't got a left foot and so when he's in possession force him on his left all the time,' the coach stressed.

'West Brom's Graham Lovett was the first to be tested by an aggressive run from Newton, and he expertly jockeyed him out to the left, making sure he was unable to switch the ball to his right foot. Then suddenly Newton let fly with a rocketing left-foot shot fom thirty yards that was a goal from the moment that he connected. It was a cracker.

'Lovett looked to the touchline bench with his arms opened wide to express his astonishment. "Thought you said he only had a right foot!" he shouted. Back came the reply: "It's the wrong bloody Newton ...!"

'The goal-scorer was KEITH Newton, England international full-back and a left-foot specialist. Henry wasn't even playing. I was a witness to Lovett's conversation with the bench, and have to say it was one of the funniest moments I ever knew on a football pitch. The look on his face had to be seen to be believed.'

BOB HILLER, a full-back famed for his kicking accuracy, was taking his time preparing to take a crucial kick for the British Lions during a tour of New Zealand. As he dug at the turf to build himself a mound on which to rest the ball, a home spectator shouted, 'Do you want a shovel, Hiller?' Bob paused, looked in the direction of the spectator and shouted back in his best Oxford University tones, 'No, your mouth will do, old chap.' He then proceeded to kick the ball between the posts before turning back to his heckler and delivering a double Harvey Smith signal.

KEN JONES, Welsh international wing three-quarter, went into a huddle with fly-half David Watkins during an international match against South Africa at Durban in 1964. Asked after the game what tactical move they had been discussing, Jones explained, 'I just told David to kick the ball down to their "25" because there was a smashing-looking bird down there.'

NOBBY STILES, the Toothless Tiger hero of England's 1966 World Cup winning team, was a notorious sleep-walker. George Eastham recalled: 'During the World Cup finals I used to have a golf club in bed with me in case Nobby attacked me. He was really frightening because he also talked while he sleep-walked. In the end, we barricaded his bed behind chairs and cases to stop him getting out.'

Thankfully, Nobby was wide awake against West Germany as he entered the land of footballing legend ... minus his teeth and with his contact lenses in place.

Nobby was as blind as the proverbial bat without his contact lenses or spectacles, and he once went 'missing' from an England after-match banquet at a swish hotel in Gothenburg.

He had left the dinner table to go to the toilet, and after he had been gone for nearly an hour the rest of the England party began to wonder whether they should send out a search party. Then a red-faced Nobby appeared, laughing as he explained where he had been. 'I left my glasses here at the table,' he said. 'When I came out of the loo I managed to walk into the banqueting suite next door. I was wandering around looking for our table, and it was ages before I realised I was at somebody's wedding reception.'

Dear old Nobby was a real Jekyll and Hyde character. Off the pitch he was quiet, likeable and God-fearing. But once he crossed the white lines with a number six shirt on his back – whether it was the red of Manchester United or the white of England – he became a tiger. A toothless tiger, of course, because he always used to leave his false teeth in the dressing-room. He was not exactly the prettiest of sights without his teeth, and a Liverpool fan once began a letter to him, 'Dear Ugly.'

Nobby was labelled a dirty player, but he never maliciously damaged anybody. He was just very, very competitive and aggressive. He got a reputation early in his career for being a vicious tackler, but it was more down to bad eyesight than any tendency towards premeditated violence.

Sir Matt Busby once caught him squinting at the team-sheet and advised him to try contact lenses. He then developed into one of the world's great midfield anchormen, but he remained a walking disaster area off the pitch. He even almost wrecked a hotel room in a sequence of accidents. He was combing his hair when the mirror over the hand basin came crashing down. When he touched panelling on the wall to see what it was made of it fell off. Then he turned on the radio and the knob came off in his hand.

Once when he was driving through Manchester his car ran into the one in front at traffic lights. He and the other driver jumped out to inspect the damage, and as they bent down they cracked their heads together.

Another time he gave relatives a lift to Manchester's Piccadilly station. After he had seen them off he discovered he had mislaid his car keys. He went through every pocket several times, then retraced his steps to the platform barrier where he had waved goodbye to his relatives. Still no sign of his keys. Finally he called a taxi and returned home for a spare set. He paid off the cabbie for the two-way journey, and then when he sat behind the wheel of his car he found the missing keys. They were still in the ignition where he had left them.

Nobby and Pat (Paddy) Crerand, both devout Catholics, went to a Mass in Madrid on the eve of Manchester

United's 1968 European Cup semi-final against Real Madrid. When Nobby put a pile of pesetas in the collection box Paddy whispered: 'It's no good trying to bribe Him, you know. We've got to win on our ability.'

The United players got a hostile reaction from Spanish fans as they left the Real Madrid ground after a memorable victory. Nobby – it had to be Nobby, of course – got clonked on the head by a bottle. Paddy Crerand waved and smiled at the supporters as they spat and screamed at the United coach. While smiling in an apparently friendly fashion, he was shouting: 'Muchos bollockos!'

WILLIE CARSON was racing towards the winning post at Pontefract with what he thought was a comfortable lead when he suddenly sensed a challenge coming on his outside. He called for a greater effort from his mount, but still he was aware of a shadow looming on his shoulder.

'I drove my horse even harder and was relieved to get past the post in first place,' said Willie. 'Then I looked behind me to see how close the other horse was. I couldn't see a thing. I'd spent the last couple of furlongs racing my own shadow. The official winning distance was fifteen lengths.'

PAT EDDERY was so keen to race through any gaps left on the rails in his early days as an apprentice jockey that Joe Mercer told him: 'I'm going to nickname you Polyfilla because you're always filling the gaps.'

TOMMY STACK, who rode Red Rum to the third of his Grand National triumphs, was asked what he said to the horse on his way round Aintree. 'I never know what to say to him,' he replied. 'You see, he's so much more intelligent than me. I just sit there and let him do the talking with his hooves.'

TERRY VENABLES was one of the cheekiest of all players. I recall when he scored what must rate as one of the most impudent goals ever netted at Stamford Bridge. He was playing for Chelsea against AS Roma in a 1965 European Fairs Cup tie, and Chelsea were awarded a free-kick ten yards outside the penalty area. Venners placed the ball as if he were going to take it and then made a great fuss of pacing out the stipulated ten yards, holding up his fingers in mime of a count as he approached Roma's defensive wall.

The Italians, duped into thinking that Venables was going to have to return to the ball, opened up the wall and allowed him through.

Suddenly Venables shouted to team-mate John Hollins: 'Give it now!' Hollins steered the ball through the hole that Terry had created in the middle of the wall, and he coolly fired a low shot into the net for one of three goals he scored that night.

Two years later, Venables was playing for Tottenham against Fulham at White Hart Lane when he got involved in a stand-up fight with Fulham defender Fred Callaghan, with whom he had grown up in Dagenham.

It was a week after Muhammad Ali had outpointed Ernie Terrell over fifteen rounds during which he kept demanding of his outclassed opponent: 'What's my name?' As Venables and Callaghan were sparring a fan shouted, 'For f***'s sake tell him your name, Venables!' Both players were ordered off for fighting. Joker Terry said later: 'We were both sent off for hitting with the inside of the glove.'

TOMMY BOLT, US Open champion in 1958, had a violent temper that earned him the nickname 'Thunderbolt'. One of his most publicised outbursts came in the US Open at Denver in 1960 when he mis-hit a shot into the pond at the twelfth.

He had a heated argument with a US PGA official as to where he should place the ball for his penalty shot, and this so upset his concentration that he three putted the next hole, bogeyed the next and hooked two drives off the eighteenth tee into a lake.

By now Bolt was in his most thunderous mood, and at the end of the round he swung his driver round his head and sent it spinning into the lake. A small boy came racing out of the crowd, dived into the lake and came out triumphantly holding the driver.

Bolt's caddie walked forward to receive it, but – to the cheers of the gallery – the boy side-stepped him and raced off into the distance clutching his prize.

MAX FAULKNER, the colourful 1951 Open champion, employed a regular caddie nicknamed 'Mad Mac', who was, to say the least, somewhat eccentric. He wore a raincoat but no shirt, and he always studied the greens through binoculars from which the lenses had been removed.

Faulkner was teeing off in a domestic tournament when

he noticed his caddie swaying as if in a strong wind. 'Are you all right?' asked Max.

'I'm as trim as a daisy,' replied the caddie in a slurred voice. 'I've just polished off a bottle of brandy, and I'll start on another one when you've won this tournament.'

Faulkner birdied the hole in two, and then looked around for the flag. His caddie was flat out on the tee, clasping the flag in his arms.

Max replaced the flag in the hole, and then half carried and half dragged the caddie behind a gorse bush where he left him sleeping like a baby.

DOUG SANDERS will always be remembered for missing a sitter of a putt that would have won him the British Open in 1970 (he went on to lose a play-off to Jack Nicklaus). He also had putting problems in the 1968 Masters when he played magnificent golf everywhere but on the greens. At the end of his round, his caddie Walter 'Cricket' Pritchett said, 'Nice work, Mister Doug. You've just managed to turn a perfect 64 into a 72!'

JACK CHARLTON won a special award from his England team-mates at the end of the triumphant 1966 World Cup campaign. Jack's name was drawn out of the hat for routine drug tests so many times that at the end of the tournament he was presented with a baby's potty with lettering on it that read 'The Jimmy Riddle Cup'.

RAY WILKINS got in a rut during his career at Manchester United when he always seemed to pass the ball sideways rather than forward. Tommy Docherty cracked, 'Ray has become the crab of football. The only time he goes forward is to spin the coin – and he even tosses that sideways.'

When a 22-yard cricket strip was being laid across the middle of the United training ground, Ron Atkinson – then the Old Trafford manager – said, 'Look, Ray, they're marking out your territory.'

SIR STANLEY ROUS, the late President of FIFA and the most influential voice British football has ever had, was England's top referee between the wars. 'I blew for a penalty in one League match and immediately realised I was wrong,' he recalled. 'As I pointed to the penalty spot the players started to protest. I strode imperiously past them and on past the goal with my finger still pointing. I then bellowed at the crowd behind the goal, "If the person who keeps blowing a whistle does not stop I shall call the police!" I then restarted play with a drop ball.'

JIM LAKER, 19-wicket hero of England's Test victory over Australia at Old Trafford in 1956, was invited by a school sports master to present the end-of-term prizes. The head teacher, who knew next to nothing about cricket, introduced him like this: 'We are delighted to have with us Mr Baker, who has got nineteen tickets for the Old Trafford Test.'

FRED TRUEMAN, England's fiery fast bowler who became a popular member of the BBC Test Match Special team, was asked how he would have punished the vandals who wrecked the pitch during the England-Australia Test at Headingley in 1975. 'I would have chucked them off the pavilion roof,' said Fred. 'But I'd have played fair, and given them a 50-50 chance of being saved. I would have had Keith Fletcher waiting below to catch them!'

BRIAN JOHNSTON, the fondly remembered clown prince of the Test Match Special team, was a notorious leg puller. On one memorable occasion during an England-Australia Test, he had just taken delivery of one of the many home-made cakes that listeners used to send in to him. He signalled to Australian co-commentator Alan McGilvray to help himself to a slice, and waited for him to take a mouthful before saying into the microphone: 'Well, that was perilously close to a catch behind the wicket. Alan McGilvray, let's have your verdict on that.' McGilvray's reply was accompanied by a spray of crumbs.

Jonners once mischievously waited for West Indian commentator Tony Cozier to join him in the commentary box, and just as he sat down and put on the headphones he ad-libbed: 'Well, that's the full statistical information on each of the England players, including their up-to-date averages. I'll now pass over to Tony Cozier for him to give us the same information about the West Indian players.'

An all-time classic moment in sports broadcasting involved Jonners and the charismatic newcomer to the Test Match Special team, Jonathan Agnew. Ian Botham had just been given out hit wicket at The Oval in 1991, and Aggers said quite innocently, 'Botham could not quite get his leg over.' This was followed by two minutes of unintelligible commentary from Jonners as he battled unsuccessfully to control a fit of the giggles. Listeners across the country were doubled up with laughter, and among the hundreds of appreciative letters they received was one from comedian Ronnie Corbett. 'It was the funniest thing I have ever heard on radio,' he wrote. 'I was at the wheel of my car, and I was laughing so much that I had to pull on to the hard shoulder of the M1.'

TOSH CHAMBERLAIN was one of the great characters on the London soccer stage during the 1950s and '60s. He was a legend in his own half-time at Fulham in the era when Johnny Haynes was the king of Craven Cottage, and Jimmy Hill was the bearded rebel without a pause who brilliantly led the players' revolt that brought the lifting of the maximum wage.

Hill and Haynes got the headlines, but it was their team-mate Tosh who got the laughs. I once saw him take a corner at Leyton Orient when he was so busy looking towards the goalmouth that he missed the ball completely and kicked the corner flag out of the ground.

Haynes and Tosh were good mates, but Haynsie used to nag the life out of Tosh on the pitch because – like most players – he could not match Johnny's perfectionist standards.

Tosh was left-wing partner to Haynes, and in one match he failed to gather a pass from the England skipper who gave him a verbal volley. 'You stupid f****** c***,' he shouted, using the common football industrial language that Graham Taylor brought to the public's attention during a Channel 4 television documentary.

Mervyn Griffiths, a highly respected referee from Wales, stopped the game and started to book Haynes for swearing. Tosh raced over to protest. 'But ref,' he said, 'he can call me a f****** c*** if he wants to. He's on *my* side. And I am a f****** c***.' The ref then booked Tosh as well.

There were times when Tosh could really turn it on and look as devastating as any winger in the League. He hit a purple patch in one particular game and kept going past his rival full-back as if he weren't there. Midway through the second half he skinned him for the umpteenth time and went on to score a spectacular goal. As he was making his way back to the half-way line, Tosh overhead the full-back mutter to a team-mate, 'If that flash bastard goes past me once more I'll break his f****** leg.'

It was a match in which Fulham were giving a young right-winger called Mickey Cross his big chance. Instead of lining up in his usual outside-left position at the re-start, Tosh switched to the right and said to Cross, 'Okay, son, I've ruined that full-back. Now you go over there and have a go.'

Ray King, former Newcastle United and Port Vale goal-keeper, shares this memory of those crazy but happy Craven Cottage days: 'I was playing for Port Vale against a Fulham team that included Bobby Robson and Johnny Haynes. The pitch was a sea of mud, and as that great Fulham character Tosh Chamberlain prepared to take a corner, one of his team-mates threw a handful of mud that hit me right between the eyes. The referee saw what happened and stopped the game. Then he licked – yes, licked – the mud out of my eyes and waved play on as if nothing had happened. Tosh came over and said that he had heard that the ref and I were just muddy good friends!'

MARK BROOKS, a golfer on the highly competitive US tour, marked his ball on the green during a Las Vegas tournament and then picked it up and tossed it to his caddie for cleaning. The caddie missed it and the ball splashed into the man-made lake alongside the green.

The rules are that you must finish the hole with the same ball that you started. Brooks was in no mood to forfeit penalty shots, and so he took off his shoes, socks, shirt and rolled up his trousers and waded into the lake looking for his ball. He fished out a dozen balls, but not one of them belonged to him. You could say he had thrown the game.

ROBERTO RIVELINO, the Brazilian with the rocket shot, scored an instant goal after just three seconds in a domestic league match between Corinthians and Rio Preto at the Bahia Stadium.

Isadore Irandir, the Preto goalkeeper, was on his knees praying for a good game when he looked up to see the ball sailing over his head into the roof of the net.

Rivelino had received the ball from the kick-off, saw Irandir on his knees and fired a 45-yard left foot shot from the centre-circle for the quickest goal on record.

He was a member of the magnificent Brazilian team that won the World Cup in such style in Mexico in 1970. Brazilian fans, many of them press photographers, reporters and radio and television interviewers, excitedly mobbed the Brazilian players after they had beaten Italy in the Final to win the Jules Rimet trophy outright. Rivelino collapsed under the weight of their congratulations, and had to be carried to the dressing-room on a stretcher.

The Jules Rimet trophy had been stolen while being exhibited in England in 1966. It was found under a hedge in a garden by a dog called Pickles. But the famous trophy disappeared for good when it was stolen while on display in Brazil. The Brazilian FA now have a replica on show.

JERRY QUARRY, former world heavyweight title challenger, knocked out British champion Jack Bodell in just 64 seconds at Wembley in 1971. In the dressing-room after his demolition job, Quarry told reporters: 'I was warned that Bodell was big and awkward, and he was. He fell very awkwardly.'

JACK DEMPSEY, who would have plenty of support as the hardest hitting heavyweight champion of all time, was once asked by a young prospect what advice he could give him as he set out on his professional career. 'Well, son, some night you'll catch a punch between the eyes and all of a sudden you'll see three guys in the ring,' said Dempsey. 'Pick out the one in the middle and hit him as hard as you can, because as sure as eggs is eggs he's the one who hit you.'

KIRKLAND LAING was not only one of the most skilful but also one of the most eccentric British fighters of modern times. I was ringside at Southend during one of his early contests under the management of champion maker Terry Lawless.

The fight was in progress when I wondered where a whistling sound was coming from. I then realised that it was Kirk who was whistling a tune as he waltzed around his outclassed opponent.

When he went back to his corner at the end of the sixth round in an eight-round contest, Lawless told him: 'If you carry on whistling and giving this fight less than 100 per cent you won't find me here when you come back at the end of the round.'

Kirk being Kirk, he carried on whistling his happy tune. When the bell ended the round, he found he had no manager left in his corner.

'I had to teach him a lesson,' said Lawless, who has a great sense of humour except when it comes to the serious business of boxing. 'The boxing ring is no place for clowning.'

But Kirk carried on clowning for much of his eventful career during which he won the British and European welterweight titles and became one of the few fighters to beat Roberto Duran near his peak.

FRANK BRUNO was standing starkers in the Royal Albert Hall dressing-room after knocking out American opponent Larry Frazier in two rounds when an eager radio reporter approached him for the naked truth.

Bruno was still dripping wet from the shower as the reporter stuck a microphone under his nose and asked: 'Tell me, Frank, what do you plan to do next?'

'Hopefully dry myself and get some clothes on,' said big Frank.

Undaunted, the man at the mike then said: 'Don't you feel it's time you were exposed to somebody in the top ten so that we can see what you're really made of?'

Bruno looked down at himself, and replied: 'Well, if you don't know now, nobody will.'

He then released that deep, booming laugh of his before adding off air: 'It's just as well that interview wasn't on television, know what I mean, Harry!'

BOB WILLIS is rarely lost for words, but he was close to it when he led the England tour team to Australia in 1982. He had practised his opening words for the press, but was not quite prepared for the first question put to him by a hard-nosed Aussie reporter: 'Welcome to Oz, Bob. What's it like to be leading the worst England team ever to reach these shores?'

FRANK TYSON was fielding in the deep after a spell during which his 'typhoon' deliveries destroyed the Australian batsmen on the 1954-55 tour. A spectator behind him shouted: 'Oi, Tyson, why don't you start bowling pianos? It's the only way they'll be able to play you.'

RAY LINDWALL kept getting the outside edge of the bat and the slip fielders kept dropping their catches during his debut for Nelson in the Lancashire League. 'Serves thee right,' shouted a spectator. 'That'll teach thee to bowl at t'bloody wickets.'

DUNCAN McKENZIE, one of the greatest entertainers of the 1970s, was never afraid to play soccer with a smile. Long after his retirement he owned up to claiming a goal he did not score. He was playing at Old Trafford when the ball floated into Manchester United's goalmouth. McKenzie – Forest, Leeds, Anderlecht and Everton were among his seven clubs – jumped head to head with United's David Sadler, who glanced the ball into his own net.

Almost before their feet touched the ground, Sadler pleaded: 'For gawd's sake, Duncan – stick your arm up and claim it!' McKenzie, now one of the funniest performers on the sporting after-dinner speaking circuit, obliged with lightning reflexes and accepted rapturous applause in the belief that one good turn deserved another.

RODNEY MARSH had a wit to match his stunning skill. When Gordon Jago took over as the new manager of Queen's Park Rangers, Rodney greeted him in the dressing-room with the comment: 'Welcome, boss. We're all behind you 50 per cent.'

JIM THORPE, a full-blooded Sac Indian from Oklahoma, won both the pentathlon and the decathlon in the 1912 Olympics in Stockholm. When the King of Sweden told him, 'Sir, you are the greatest athlete in the world,' Thorpe replied, 'Thanks, King.'

MIRUTS YIFTER was one of the favourites for the 5,000 metres in the 1972 Munich Olympics, but when the runners lined up for the heats he was nowhere to be seen. He was later found in tears at the trackside, explaining that when the athletes had been called to the mark he was locked in the toilet. Four years later he missed the Montreal Games because of the African boycott, but he got his long overdue golden glory in 1980 when winning both the 5,000 and 10,000 metres in the Moscow Olympics. The Ethiopian father of six was quite flushed with success!

There was a mystery about Yifter's age, and he admitted at various times to being 33, 35, 36, 37 and 42. When asked to put the record straight, he said: 'I have never gone in for counting the years. Men may steal my chickens, men may steal my sheep. But no man can steal my age.'

SEBASTIAN COE was in the warm-up area preparing for his first major challenge in a British international vest. It was the European Indoor Championships at San Sebastian in 1971. All around him coaches were shouting advice and instructions to their charges. Coe waited and wondered what British team manager Bob Stinson would find to say to him in the moments before his vital 800 metres race.

When the runners were called to the arena, Stinson looked at Coe and said simply, 'Well, bye-bye then.'

Coe won the title in 1min. 46.5secs., just a tenth of a second outside the world indoor record.

STEVE OVETT, Coe's great rival virtually throughout their track careers, was having what he described as 'mental and spiritual' problems at one stage early in his development. He said, 'I should wear one of those car stickers that read, "Don't follow me, I'm lost."'

BILL SHANKLY, whose name will always live on at Anfield as the 'Liverpool Legend', took his team to Germany for a pre-season friendly match. Tommy Smith had let rip with several of his famed and feared tackles. The German referee felt moved to come into the Liverpool dressing-room at half-time and said to Shanks in broken English, 'Smith – number four – one bad tackle more – off!'

Shanks digested this and replied in broken Scottish: 'Smith – if he off – everybody off!'

Shanks idolised his old Preston team-mate Tom Finney, and called him the greatest thing on two feet. He used to say that Finney could run rings round a defence while wearing an overcoat. Somebody once made the mistake of saying in Bill's hearing that Mike Summerbee was almost as good as Finney.

'Aye,' said Shanks. 'You're right there. Summerbee IS almost as good as Finney, but you've got to remember that Tom is now 62.'

JEFF ASTLE, former England and West Brom centre-forward, was a very witty bloke who always had a joke up his sleeve. When he went to a bullfight in Mexico during the 1970 World Cup he was asked by Francis Lee if he'd fight one of the bulls for £1,000.

'Fight it?' said Jeff. 'For a thousand pounds I'd milk the f*****g thing.'

That season West Brom bought Tranmere goalkeeper Jim Cumbes for £30,000. Jim was better known as a fast-medium bowler with Lancashire, Surrey and, later, Worcestershire. When Astle was told that the club were buying

Cumbes, he said: 'The club must be f*****g mad. For another ten thousand quid they could have got John Snow.'

JIMMY HILL likes to ride his horse, a hunter, when he's not working on television or overseeing things at Craven Cottage in his capacity as Fulham chairman. He claims that he was sitting astride his horse one day waiting for a hunt to start when his horse loudly broke wind. Jimmy was talking to an aristocratic lady at the time and, rather embarrassed, said, 'I'm sorry about that, your ladyship.' 'Oh, that's all right,' she said in a plummy voice. 'I thought it was the horse.'

VIRGINIA WADE had just won the women's championship in the 1977 Wimbledon Centenary year. Everybody wanted to know at the press conference afterwards: 'What did the Queen have to say to you?' Virginia shrugged and said, 'I wish I could tell you, but the noise from the crowd was so deafening I was unable to hear. But it was just great to see her lips moving.'

DR RENEE RICHARDS holds the unique record of having competed in both the men's and women's tournaments in the US tennis championships. In 1960, then answering to the name of Richard Raskind, he was beaten 6-0, 6-1, 6-1 in the first round by Neale Fraser. Following a sex change operation in 1977, she competed as Renée Richards, and was beaten 6-1, 6-4 in the first round by Virginia Wade. 'I am on a quest to prove that trans-sexuals can hold their heads up high,' said Dr Richards.

JOE NAMATH, idolised New York Jets quarter-back, played in the first match on Astroturf after American football had begun to switch from traditional grass. At the press conference after the match on the synthetic surface, Joe was asked: 'What's the difference between grass and Astroturf?'

'Well,' drawled Joe, 'I can't rightly say 'cos I've never smoked Astroturf.'

BRIAN CLOSE was famed throughout the cricket world for being the toughest of all competitors. This story from England cricket supremo Ray Illingworth explains why: 'I was bowling for Yorkshire against Gloucestershire skipper Martin Young in a County match. Martin went down on one knee to play a sweep shot. He really middled the ball and it went like a bullet and hit Brian Close on the forehead straight between the eyes.

'Brian was fielding at short leg in the days before helmets. The ball bounced from his head back over the top of Martin Young, over the head of our wicket-keeper Jimmy Binks and into the hands of Philip Sharpe at first slip. As Brian was being taken to the dressing-room for treatment he was arguing that he should be credited with the catch!'

I contacted Martin Young at his home in South Africa to add to the story. He told me, 'I went into the Yorkshire dressing-room to see Brian receiving treatment. The doctor said, "Count yourself lucky. I dread to think what would have happened had the ball hit you behind the ear."

'Brian, nursing an egg-size bump, considered this and then replied, "He would have been caught at cover instead of at slip." They bred them tough in our day.'

Close is a low-handicap, ambidextrous golfer, who always takes his will-to-win attitude on to the course. He once played in a four-ball that included his former Yorkshire and England team-mate Fred Trueman. Close was having a nightmare round, and after slicing three successive balls into a lake at the twelfth hole he picked up his bag and trolley and hurled them into the water.

Then, according to the Trueman version of the story, he walked off the course without a word to his partners.

Ten minutes later Trueman looked up from the tee to see Close walking back towards him. 'I thought he was coming to apologise for his behaviour,' said Fred. 'But that's never been his style. He walked past us on the way back to the lake, muttering, "I can't get into t'bloody car. My keys are in t'golf bag.'

Close then removed his shoes and socks, rolled up his trousers and waded into the lake in search of the bag that he had consigned to a watery grave.

ARTHUR MAILEY, one of the most successful of all Australian bowlers and later respected as a philosopher on the game, had a finely tuned sense of humour. He finished with figures of 4 for 362 when playing for New South Wales in the famous match in which Victoria scored 1,107 runs. Mailey said later: 'I would have had even more impressive figures if a bloke wearing a brown trilby sitting in the sixth row of the pavilion stand had not dropped two catches.'

WILLIE PASTRANO, former world light-heavyweight champion, had just climbed up at the count of nine in a bruising battle against José Torres. As the referee brushed his gloves and looked into his eyes, he shouted: 'D'you know where you are, Willie?' Pastrano replied through bleeding lips, 'You bet I know where I am. I'm in Madison Square Garden and I'm getting beaten up.'

ROCKY MARCIANO, who remains the only world heavyweight champion to have retired without a single defeat on his record, made a comeback of sorts six months before his death in a plane crash. He was persuaded to

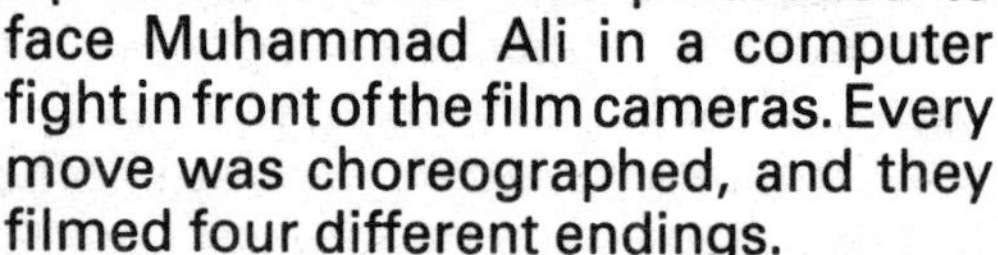

face Muhammad Ali in a computer fight in front of the film cameras. Every move was choreographed, and they filmed four different endings.

They put a wig on Rocky's balding head, and hid his bulging stomach in a pair of specially tailored shorts. 'Hey, d'ya know somethin'?' Rocky said as a make-up artist fitted his hairpiece. 'This rug cost more than I got for my first professional fight.'

Marciano died the day before his 49th birthday without knowing the result of the phantom fight. A week later the film was released with the version showing him stopping Ali in the tenth round. Ali said later, 'I went along with it out of respect to Rocky's memory, but the truth is that at my peak he would not have been able to hit me with a handful of rice.'

Ali had a quote for every occasion, but even he was almost lost for words when he heard the size of the alimony cheque he would have to pay his first wife, Sonja, following their divorce in 1967. 'I'm the only one to beat him,' said Sonja. 'He's going to remember that every day for the next ten years while he's making the payments.'

When he got his senses back, Ali said: 'I'm having to pay so much money that they've even named the payments after me – *Ali*mony!'

JIM WATT, who with ITV's Voice of Boxing Reg Gutteridge forms the best commentary double act on television, was one of the wittiest as well as shrewdest boxers to win a world title for Britain. I worked as a publicist on his final title fight against the brilliant Alexis Arguello at Wembley, and after his points defeat sat alone with him in his hotel bathroom while he soaked out the bruises of battle. Jim, whose business away from boxing was buying and selling cars at a garage that he owned in Glasgow, looked at his swollen face in the mirror and said: 'If this was a motor car, I'd have to describe it as a write-off.'

BRIAN CLOUGH is one of the most astonishing characters that I have met in my sportswriting career, and his self-belief as both a manager and player was in the Ali class. As a magnificent goal striker with Middlesbrough and Sunderland, he always considered himself superior to just about everybody he played with or against. A team-mate once complained because he had pushed him off the ball in the penalty area and then banged it into the net. 'Well, I'm better at scoring than you are,' was Cloughie's matter-of-fact explanation.

He adopted this 'I am the greatest' attitude as a manager, and proceeded to put action where his mouth was. After collecting the European Cup for a second successive season with Nottingham Forest, he said: 'If we'd entered we'd have won the bloomin' Boat Race, too!'

Cloughie once paid new signing Billy Stubbs a £10 bonus for shaving off his moustache. 'I don't want a 20-year-old walking round the club looking older than the manager,' he said.

DENIS LAW, he of the electric heels and lightning reflexes, scored six goals for Manchester City in an FA Cup tie against Luton before the match was abandoned because of a waterlogged pitch. As they trudged off, the referee apologised to Denis for having to call off the game. 'Och, I'm used to it,' said the Law man. 'The same thing happened to me in a schools game in Scotland. As soon as I score six goals, the heavens open.' When the Cup tie was replayed Denis scored again, but City lost 2-1. Seven goals and he had finished on the losing side!

IAN ST JOHN plays the straight man to Jimmy Greaves, but can be very funny in his own right. The Saint was playing in a charity match organised by his London Weekend Television colleague Jim Rosenthal, and was persuaded during the game to take a penalty. It was the only time in his entire career that he had taken a spot-kick, and he thumped the ball against a post. Straight faced, the Saint told his team-mates: 'I aimed for the post because I wanted to maintain my 100 per cent record.'

The Saint passes on this story about a great Everton character, Sandy Brown, who was a popular defender at Goodison during Ian's days as the king of the Kop at Anfield: 'There was a competition being organised to find the hardest shot in the country. Sandy prided himself on his kicking power, and the Everton lads wound him up by saying that they wanted him to represent the club in the competition. They told him that they would test out the speed of his shot during a break at their training ground.

'A ball was put on the halfway line and Alex Young arranged for a car to be revved up just beyond the touch-line. "The way we'll measure the speed of your shot is to see if you can get the ball into the net before the car reaches the goal-line," Sandy was told by that great leg-puller Alex.

'So with the car careering along the touch-line, he kept banging the ball towards the net until they told him he was still short of the 90 miles per hour that Peter Lorimer had recorded at Leeds. It was six or seven shots before Sandy realised he was being taken for a ride.'

It was Sandy who, during an Everton tour in the United States, walked into a New York bar and said in his best James Bond voice: 'Scotch on the rocks, no ice.'

PAUL GASCOIGNE became the modern clown prince of football with his antics on the pitch with Newcastle, Tottenham and then Lazio. His humour was not exactly subtle. He upset a television interviewer when he burped into his microphone, pulled down the shorts of a colleague who was holding aloft a trophy at the time, and smelt under a referee's armpits while an England international match was in full flow.

It was the tears of a clown that brought him his greatest exposure when he cried following England's penalties defeat by Germany in the 1990 World Cup finals. Gazza had his team-mates crying with laughter during a match against Hungary when, every time the Hungarian marking him tried to make a tackle, he stuck his tongue out at him. No wonder Bobby Robson described him as being 'as daft as a brush'.

LEN SHACKLETON, another North East idol, was the original clown prince, and Gazza was brought up on tales of Shack's party tricks. He used to get up to such things as sitting on the ball, shaking hands with the corner flag, dancing with referees and making opponents look fools by spinning the ball around them and through their legs.

Shack's eccentricity frightened the establishment and he was awarded a miserly six England caps. Walter Winterbottom was the England manager at the time. He was an intellectual who did not deliver tactical talks as much as lectures. He was once chalking on a blackboard the path he wanted Stan Mortensen and Shack to follow on the way through a defence. 'You, Morty,' said Walter, 'can take the ball to here, then pass it to Shack here. Shack can move to here before making a return pass to Morty here. Then Shack must get here for the return pass before steering the ball into the net. Any questions, gentlemen?'

Shack said: 'Just one, boss. Which side of the net do you want me to put it?'

JIMMY WHITE used to spend more time at the snooker table than the school desk when he was a kid, and by the time he was 13 could pick up more in one side bet than his teacher could earn in a year. I learned this from the man who knew best of all, his actual teacher, who came on as a guest on a *This Is Your Life* tribute to Jimmy that I scripted. 'It got to the stage,' said the teacher, 'where I did a deal with Jimmy. I told him that provided he came to school for the morning lessons I would let him off in the afternoons to play snooker. It was hardly a thing the school board would have gone along with, but at least this way I managed to get Jimmy behind a desk for part of the day. Without that deal we would never have seen him!'

STEVE DAVIS has played up to his 'interesting' image, but has in fact got a nicely developed line in dry humour. He once reduced a camera crew and director to helpless laughter when recording a snooker instruction programme.

'This is the ideal place to hit the pack with the cue ball when breaking off,' he said, then gave the demonstration. The ball glanced the pack, ran down to the bottom cushion and spun into a corner pocket. Steve looked direct into the camera and said, 'Here endeth the lesson and Steve Davis's television career.'

JOHN VIRGO, famous for his Big Break appearances and his impressions at the table, was competing in a televised match against Cliff 'The Grinder' Thorburn when he was played into a virtually impossible snooker. John shook his head as he studied the balls, and said: 'I've not yet quite mastered an impression of Houdini.'

RAY REARDON, nicknamed Dracula because he only comes out at night, has brightened snooker with his humour. He was once involved in a marathon match with Fred 'Smiler' Davis when water dripped on to the table from a leaking roof. 'This is a hard slog, Fred,' he said. 'Even the balls are sweating.'

WILL CARLING, England Rugby captain, could not be missed as he sat at the team lunch table during a training get-together with the international squad. A snooker cue had been pushed through the sleeves of his jacket, and he looked like an umpire signalling a wide. The entire team then watched him try to sup his soup of the day. This was Will's punishment for being voted the worst performer in that morning's training session.

WADE DOOLEY, England's huge second-row forward, was celebrating a victory over France in the Moulin Rouge night-club in Paris. Dooley had been one of England's most prominent players, coming out on top in a fierce battle with his French counterparts. One of the cabaret acts featured a circus strongman wrestling with two crocodiles. 'Look,' came a shout from one of Dooley's teammates. 'It's an action replay of Wade in the loose mauls against France.'

BOB PAISLEY told me the following story in the days when he was collecting every trophy in sight as manager at Liverpool, for whom he had been a solid midfield player: 'Liverpool were playing Huddersfield in a League match in the late 1940s. Those were the days when referees used to leave the match ball on the centre-spot at half-time because spectators knew their place and would not dare put a foot on the sacred turf.

'We came out and lined up for the start of the second half, and it was Huddersfield to kick off. I can see it now as clearly as if it were yesterday – the great Peter Doherty, wearing the number ten shirt for Huddersfield, jogging up and down in anticipation as he waited for his centre-forward to tap the ball to him.

'The whistle blew and off we went. Peter was quickly away on one of those magical weaving runs of his, and he was ghosting through our defence when suddenly the whistle went for no apparent reason.

'We looked up in bewilderment to see the ref and his two linesmen approaching the pitch from the players' tunnel. The ref was blowing a Harry James trumpet solo on his whistle to get us to stop the game, so that he could get on.

'We had managed to start the game without him thanks to a wag in the crowd who had a whistle with him!'

RON FLOWERS, blond, strapping Wolves defender, was on an England summer tour in the 1960s. As he walked out of the stadium after a match that England had won, an elderly international selector – smart in his England blazer – shook him by the hand. 'You played a blinder, son, and have got a big future in an England shirt,' he said. 'When we get back to the hotel I'll buy you a celebration drink, Bobby.'

Jimmy Greaves, standing alongside, was bent double with laughter as the selector toddled off. 'He thinks you're Bobby Moore,' he said to the bewildered Flowers, who had not even played in the match.

SIR BOBBY CHARLTON, British football's greatest ambassador, pitched in with this memory of Duncan Edwards, his Manchester United team-mate who tragically died in the horrific 1958 Munich air disaster that Bobby thankfully survived:

'Duncan was *the* complete player. Good with both feet, strong in the tackle, commanding in the air, a powerful shot and an accurate passer of the ball no matter what the distance. He could play in any position, and he had the ability to dictate and dominate any match, as this story will illustrate.

'I remember a particular game when I was playing with Duncan for the Army against the RAF during our National Service. Duncan received the ball from our goalkeeper deep in our half, passed it to the full-back and took the return pass. Then he exchanged passes with me, passed it to another forward, quickly demanded it back and unleashed the hardest shot you're ever likely to see. The ball rocketed towards the goalkeeper's head from the edge of the box. He ducked out of the way, and the ball flashed into the net.

'Quite a few years later I was walking down a street in Cambridgeshire when a chap stopped me. "You don't remember me, do you, Bobby?" he said. "I played against you some years back when I was in the RAF and you were in the Army team." As the game came back into my memory, I asked him which position he played. "Goalie," he said. When I laughed and reminded him how he had ducked out of the way of Duncan's shot, he replied, "Yes, that was the proudest moment of my life."'

SIR COLIN COWDREY, one of cricket's gentlemen, was given a violent introduction to cricket's ruthless modern era when he was called up as a reinforcement at the age of 42 on England's torrid tour of Australia in 1974-75. Just four days after his arrival Down Under, Cowdrey was picked to play in the second Test on a lightning fast Perth pitch against the lethal Aussie fast bowling team of Jeff Thomson and Dennis Lillee. At the fall of the first English wicket Cowdrey entered the cauldron to join Lancastrian David Lloyd in the middle. He was greeted with a barrage of hostile bouncers which whistled past his ears and a tirade of colourful language from Thomson. At the end of the over, Lloyd strolled down the wicket to give some encouragement to his pilloried partner only to be greeted by a grinning Cowdrey who enthused: "I say, old chap, this is awfully good fun isn't it?!"

TREVOR BAILEY, one of England's most outstanding all-rounders in the immediate post-war years, happily recalls the day he clean bowled his Australian counterpart Keith Miller for a duck while bowling for Essex against Don Bradman's 1948 tourists at Southchurch Park, Southend. That's the good news. The bad news is that the Australians amassed an all-time record 712 runs in one day. They were all out, the only time on that tour that every Aussie batsman was dismissed.

Miller, an old *Daily Express* colleague of mine, later confided that he deliberately surrendered his wicket because he did not like the slaughter that was going on in the name of sport. Keith received an unusual honour for his non-scoring performance. He was invited to join the Pygmalion Duck Club, formed by broadcaster John Arlott for batsmen considered to have collected 'a distinguished duck'.

JOHN ARLOTT was the master of the microphone who enchanted millions of radio listeners with his poetic view of cricket. When England captain George Mann hit South African left-arm spinner Tufty Mann for six during an Arlott commentary, he described it as 'a case of Mann's inhumanity to Mann'.

RAY SMITH, Essex all-rounder of the 1950s, suggested at a team meeting that any player getting 'a pair' – two ducks in a match – should be awarded a special tie. They designed the tie there and then, two yellow ducks on a plain blue background. It was also agreed that it should be worn on the first day of every match throughout the following year on pain of having to buy drinks all round.

In the next match Smith collected a king-size pair, first-ball ducks against Surrey.

SONNY RAMADHIN, better known for his bowling than his batting, came to the wicket for the West Indies in British Guyana in 1953 following a crowd riot during which bottles had been thrown at the England fielders.

It was agreed between the players that it would be safest not to field near the boundaries. Tom Graveney, standing at slip, said to Ramadhin as he reached the middle: 'Sonny, if you hit a four you've got to go and get the ball yourself!'

SEVERIANO BALLESTEROS was a newcomer to the professional circuit when he said for public consumption, 'I cannot believe that anybody who plays golf full-time could possibly score double figures on one hole. It will never happen to me.'

The next day in the Spanish Open, the super-confident teenager hooked his drive out of bounds at the par five, 505-metres ninth hole. He again sliced his drive out of bounds, and eventually reached the fairway with five strokes to his name. He pushed his sixth shot into a water hazard, and then hit the new ball into a bunker. Seve was on the green in nine shots, and two putted to finish in an 'impossible' eleven.

JULIUS BOROS, son of a Hungarian immigrant and winner of the US Open in 1952, was asked when he reached the age of fifty if he was contemplating retirement. Boros, a keen angler, said: 'What on earth would I find to do if I retire? All I'm interested in is fishing and golfing.'

BOBBY CLAMPETT, American amateur champion who became a successful professional, missed the cut in the 1979 US Open, and was asked to go out at the start of the third round to act as a marker.

Joker Clampett decided to turn his path-finding work into an exhibition. He dropped on his knees on the first tee and fired the ball 230 yards down the fairway. The US PGA officials were unimpressed and warned Clampett to behave himself.

He could not resist clowning, and at the eleventh hole he repeated his on-the-knees drive and then putted backwards between his legs using a wedge. Before he could tee off at the twelfth he was ordered to leave the course. 'Hell, what's wrong with a little entertainment?' asked Clampett.

BJORN BORG had the distant help of his grandfather when he won the French Open in 1977. His 73-year-old grandfather listened to the final on radio while sitting in a fishing boat near Sweden's Kattilo Island. He spat nervously into the water when he won his first point, and decided with illogical superstition that this had helped his grandson. From then on he spat after every winning point, and had a bone-dry throat by the time Bjorn had beaten Victor Pecci in four sets.

JOHN McENROE surpassed himself on his way to defeat by Stefan Edberg in the 1992 Wimbledon championships. He swore at a linesman six times in ten seconds, an outburst that was picked up by an ITN microphone. This is a censored version of what shocked millions of TV viewers heard: 'Blank, you stupid blanker. Good blanking call, you son of a blanking bitch.' It cost McEnroe a maximum $10,000 fine, which worked out at $1,000 a second.

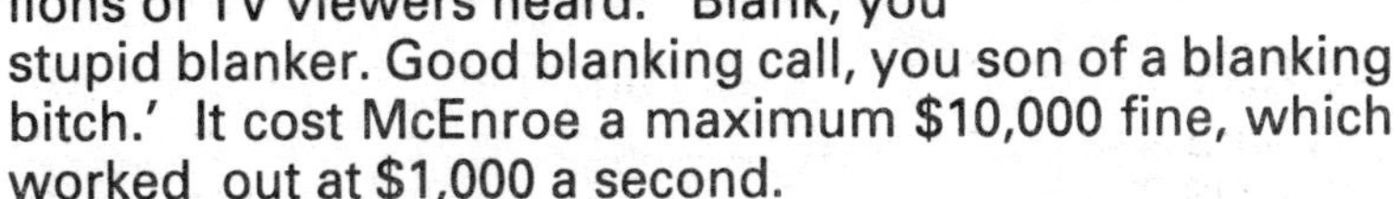

JIMMY CONNORS, the big-hearted street fighter of the tennis courts, was in the McEnroe class with his tongue during the 1992 US Open. Following a disputed line call,

he yelled at the umpire: 'You son of a bitch. Get out of that chair and get a job. I'm out here playing my butt off at 39, and you're pulling that crap.'
Anyone for tennis?

TOMMY SMITH – according to Bill Shankly – wasn't born, but was quarried out of Liverpool's Scotland Road pavement. Tommy admitted at the end of his eventful career that he had spent twelve months building his tough guy image and twelve years trying to live it down.

He had a superstition that before every major match he had to wrap his false teeth in a strip of bandage and hand them to trainer Ronnie Moran. Immediately after the final whistle, he was always the first person Tommy would look for so that he could have his teeth in for the photographers and – when necessary – for after-match presentations.

After a superb Smithy goal had helped Liverpool win the European Cup Final in Rome in 1977 he made his usual trek towards the touchline to collect his teeth from the tracksuited Moran.

The ecstatic trainer hoisted Tommy in the air, and there was a memorable photograph published which everybody thought captured Smithy celebrating the victory. In actual fact at the time the picture was taken he was saying to Ronnie Moran, 'Put me down, you big soft bugger. I want me bloody teeth!'

DIXIE DEAN, the old Everton hero, had a leg amputated late in his life, and went to a rehabilitation centre where there were a dozen invalids minus limbs. 'Blimey,' said Dixie in his Scouse accent, 'has Tommy Smith been let loose in here?'

GORDON BANKS, former England goalkeeping master, recalls a penalty by Jimmy Greaves that left him feeling anything but a saint: 'It was one of the craziest goals I ever conceded. Spurs were awarded a penalty against Leicester on a muddy pitch at White Hart Lane. There was hardly any grass around and I had gone back inside the goal to wipe all the muck off my hands ready to face the penalty. Jimmy, the cheeky sod, side-footed the ball into the other corner of the net while I was bending down. I don't know who was more surprised when the referee signalled a goal, Jimmy or me. What made it worse was that instead of telling the ref he was wrong, even my team-mates were rolling about laughing.'

MALCOLM ALLISON, recognised throughout football as one of the most accomplished of all coaches, tells this amusing story of when he was manager at Crystal Palace, with Terry Venables as his right-hand man: 'Terry and I went to Darlington to watch their League match against Doncaster with a view to buying a player.

'The Darlington directors gave us the full VIP treatment. There we were, two flash Londoners playing the big "I am" and the Darlington people couldn't do enough for us because they thought we might be spending some money on one of their players.

'When it was time for the kick-off we were shown to the best seats in the house, right in the front row of the directors' box. We sat on converted cinema seats that had been bought from a bankrupt picture palace. Many people in the crowd, curious as to what we were doing in Darlington, kept looking at us more than at the game.

'Suddenly there was a cracking noise, and our seats collapsed under us. Terry and I were left sitting on the ground looking over the top of the directors' box like a couple of Chad characters. Everybody roared with laughter to see the two "flash Harrys" brought down to earth with a bump.

'Terry and I looked at each other with one of those "That's another fine mess you've got me into, Stanley" stares and then self-consciously picked ourselves up and moved to seats at the back of the box. After that we always claimed that we brought the house down in Darlington.'

RON ATKINSON is known throughout the game as 'Big Ron' just as Malcolm Allison is known to all as 'Big Mal'. Both are larger-than-life characters. When he was manager of West Brom, Atkinson went with the then Birmingham City manager Jim Smith to the theatre to see comedian Billy Connolly, who was appearing in Brum.

After the show they were invited into the Big Yin's dressing-room. Smithy asked Billy if he found it easy to communicate with Midland audiences.

'Och aye,' said Billy. 'I enjoy playing Birmingham.'

'Don't we all,' said Big Ron. 'Don't we all.'

NICK FALDO was getting a lot of stick from the media for his morose manner on the American golf circuit, and he decided he should do something to improve his public relations. On every page of his yardage chart for the 1989 US Masters his caddie Andy Prodger had written, 'Be patient. Keep smiling.' Faldo smiled his way to the title.

IAN WOOSNAM was wondering aloud how he could improve his image as he watched the 'Great White Shark' Greg Norman grabbing the headlines on the American circuit. 'Perhaps I should try dying my hair peroxide blond,' he said. 'Then I could call myself the great white tadpole.'

LIANG-HIAN LU, the golfer who captured the public imagination as the gentlemanly 'Mr Lu' in the 1971 British Open at Royal Birkdale, hooked a shot into the gallery. His ball hit a woman spectator and she was taken to hospital for treatment.

At the end of his round, Mr Lu visited the woman in hospital and presented her with a box of half a dozen golf balls. 'Now,' he said, 'you throw at me.'

JOE LOUIS had such quick reflexes in his peak years that his favourite trick was catching flies in mid-flight. He could throw his punches with similar lightning speed. During his 'Bum-a-month' campaign he fought a loud New York bartender called 'Two Ton' Tony Galento. Nearly as wide as he was tall, Tony was a boxing promoter's dream and could talk a much better fight than he could actually fight.

He made world-wide headlines with his boast that he would 'moider da bum' when he climbed into the ring with Louis. As the referee helped Galento off the canvas after he had been flattened in four rounds, Galento shouted out defiantly through swollen lips, 'I'll *still* moider da bum.'

Louis revealed after the fight, 'Even as I was landing my hardest punches and sinking my fists into his ample stomach, he was saying to me, "I'll moider ya, ya bum." He sure is a funny guy.'

What 'Two Ton' Tony did do was put bums on seats.

JACK DEMPSEY said to his wife after his first shock defeat by Gene Tunney, 'Honey, I forgot to duck.' President Ronald Reagan borrowed the line when Nancy visited him in hospital after a bullet from a would-be assassin hit him sixty years later.

GEORGE FOREMAN is being turned into a television comedy actor in the United States. Ol' George won't need a scriptwriter. Here are just a few of his priceless lines during his second coming as a heavyweight fighter:

'Evander Holyfield has a nutritionist. Me, I have room service.'

'I believe that it should be made mandatory that all fighters retire at sixty-five.'

'When a promoter comes seeking my services, my first question is always, "Can ya afford to feed me as well as pay me? You ain't seen no hungry fighter like this hungry fighter."'

'I've been put on this earth to preach the Lord's word. God has given me boxing to use as bait to catch the fish.'

'The critics said my opponent was no good after I'd knocked him out. Yeah, well I'd hit him in the ribs and then I'd hit him in the head. That's why he was no good.'

'I really mean it when I say that all boxers are basically good guys. Even Mike Tyson? Yeah, Mike included. There's good in Mike deep down – deep, deep, DEEP down, deep, deep, deep, DEEP down.'

CHRIS EUBANK, the monocled mutineer, took a call at home from British Boxing Board of Control Secretary John Morris. 'Ah, you're just the man,' said Chris, without waiting to hear what John had to say. 'Just listen to this.' Eubank then played a five-minute aria by Joan Sutherland over the telephone. Chris then came back to the phone and said, 'Now, that's what you call class.' Then he put down the receiver, leaving John not knowing whether he was on his elbow or his aria.

EMIL ZATOPEK, the legendary middle and long distance runner who was a triple gold medallist in the 1952 Olympics, won his first Olympic gold medal in London in 1948. Forty years later I devised and wrote with the master of the microphone, Brian Moore, an ITV documentary called *The Games of '48*. Emil was one of our guests who came over to reminisce on the London Olympics, and the programme producer, John D. Taylor, asked him why he always looked in such agony when he ran. 'I am afraid that I was not talented enough to run and laugh at the same time,' said Emil.

The 'Bouncing Czech' – as he was dubbed by supreme sportswriter Peter Wilson – told us a story that was not reported at the time of his triumph in the 10,000 metres in the 1948 Games. He took his prized gold medal to show it to Dana, then his girlfriend, who was competing for Czechoslovakia in the javelin. The men and women were housed in different hotels and were not allowed to fraternise. But Emil did not let a little thing like a garden wall stand between him and Dana, who was later to become his wife. (They were born on the same day, incidentally, and Dana won a gold medal in the 1952 Games on the same day that Emil won the marathon.)

Anyway, Emil shinned over the wall and stood by the

swimming pool throwing pebbles up at Dana's window to attract her attention. When she looked out, he spun his medal on the ribbon around his head. It slipped out of his hand and into the pool, and he had collected quite an audience by the time he had stripped off, dived in and recovered his precious prize.

PETER SNELL, New Zealand's master middle distance runner of the 1960s, was reported to have been nearly tripped up by a rabbit when breaking the world half-mile record on a grass track in Christchurch in 1962. Snell could not understand how the story had spread until it was revealed that an agency report had referred to him side-stepping his hare (pacemaker) on the way to the record.

JESSE OWENS, arguably the greatest sprinter of all time, had not lost his speed even in middle-age. He came out of his Chicago office one day to find a thief attempting to break into his car. Jesse gave the thief a fifty yards' start, and caught him a block away from the crime. As he handed the man over to the police, the thief said: 'Can you believe it? Only I could have picked on a car belonging to the fastest man in the world.'

JIM LANGLEY, capped by England as an attack-minded left-back, was one of a host of marvellous characters at Fulham in the 1950s and 1960s. He was famed for his sliding tackles and good sportsmanship, but there was one match in which he lost his happy-go-lucky mood. He was so upset by biting half-time criticism from skipper Johnny Haynes that he refused to go out for the second half (and this was in the days before substitutes). Haynes returned to the dressing-room when he realised Langley was adamant about not continuing, and he had to apologise. He found Jim sitting in the bath. He was the cleanest player on the pitch when he rejoined the game.

Another bathtime story involved Harry Wright, goalkeeper understudy to the great Sam Bartram at Charlton Athletic. Harry was a compulsive practical joker whose favourite trick was to push fully dressed clubmates into the plunge bath in the dressing-room at The Valley.

While he was out finishing a training session one morning, another player put on Harry's suit and positioned himself in front of the bath so that Harry would see him as soon as he came into the dressing-room.

Harry couldn't resist it, and he pushed the player – and his own suit – into the bath.

PETER DOHERTY, genius of an inside-forward and later manager of Northern Ireland, had a merciless wit. While playing for Derby in the immediate post-war years, Doherty – whose son, Paul, is Head of Sport at Granada Television – came up against a defender who tried to goad him with his tongue.

'Call yourself a footballer?' taunted the defender. 'How did you win any international caps?'

At about that moment Doherty received the ball, beat the defender all ends up with a blinding bit of skill and then called over his shoulder, 'I keep getting picked for Ireland because I'm playing against idiots like you every week.'

When Doherty was manager of Northern Ireland, he once sat playing cards with his players late at night on the eve of an international match against Scotland. 'The Scottish players will have been in bed hours ago,' said one critic.

'I'm sure they were,' said Doherty, without glancing up

from his cards. 'But are they sleeping or are they tossing and turning and worrying about the game? All my players are worried about at the moment is what I'm holding in my hand.'

DANNY BLANCHFLOWER, Northern Ireland's captain when Doherty was manager, had an equally sharp wit. As captain of Tottenham in the 1961 FA Cup Final at Wembley, Danny was introducing the Duchess of Kent to the players.

'Tell me,' said the Duchess, 'why is it the Leicester players have their names on the backs of their tracksuits while your team do not?'

'Well, you see, ma'am,' said Danny, 'we all know each other.'

FRANCIS (FRANNY) LEE, the former Manchester City player who liked the club so much that he bought it, was a joker in the Maine Road pack during his playing days. On a flight back from Australia after a club tour, manager Joe Mercer was a victim of one of Franny's wicked hoaxes.

He summoned a stewardess and asked her to pass a note to Joe, who was sitting at the front of the plane away from the players. When Joe opened the note it read, 'Please do not panic or react in any way, but we have reason to believe that the man sitting next to you is a hijacker. Please watch him carefully until we can get some assistance to you without upsetting any of the other passengers.' The note was signed 'The Captain'.

The City players then had the entertainment of watching Joe sit frozen in his seat trying to watch his neighbour out of the corner of his eye.

The joke ended with an explosion of laughter from the players. Dear old Joe acknowledged that he had been 'taken' with a wave of his fist in Franny's direction. Then he ordered a large drink.

PETER OSGOOD, Chelsea and England centre-forward, could always be counted on for a laugh. Once, along with clubmates Terry Venables and George Graham, he posed as customs officers at an airport. They looked the part in their blue Chelsea blazers, so much so that they managed to persuade an American tourist to open her case and declare what she was bringing into the country.

The Chelsea boys were always pulling David Webb's leg over his rugged, Desperate Dan appearance. They arrived in Amsterdam on the eve of a European match, and as they got off the coach at their hotel Ossie noticed that the front window displayed a replica of a jungle scene, with exotic plants, stuffed animals and bamboo poles. He turned to Webby and said, 'They've got your room ready, Dave!'

MARTIN PIPE is one of the outstanding racehorse trainers of modern times, but even he could not have matched the ingenuity of his wife, Carol, during a meeting at Taunton in 1993. The Pipe stable were running Elite Reg, and just before he was due to go down to the start it was discovered that his tongue strap was missing. Carol dashed to the ladies, slipped off her tights and these were used to hold down the horse's tongue. Alas, all to no avail. Elite Reg was pulled up. The jockey allegedly claimed that he had found the course too tight.

FREDDIE STARR was said to have his tongue in his cheek when Miinnehoma won the 1994 Grand National for him. The comedian had bought him at Doncaster Sales for 35,000 guineas, making his bids by sticking out his tongue at the auctioneer!

STEVE DONOGHUE, one of the most successful jockeys

of the century, was carrying extra weight when he piloted Humorist to victory in the 1921 Derby. While waiting for the 'off' he had been served with a writ for an alleged unpaid debt. He calmly tucked the writ in his silks, and proceeded to ride one of his greatest races.

NIGEL MANSELL has a nice relaxed sense of humour away from the tension of the Grand Prix circuit. I scripted his *This Is Your Life* tribute, and after being hit with the Big Red Book he kept pinching Michael Aspel to make sure he wasn't dreaming it!

Nigel is a king prankster, but was on the receiving end at a sponsor's banquet in Zandvoort. As the strawberries and cream dessert was served, the late Colin Chapman winked at John Player's Special Events Manager David Way, and said, 'Careful of the cream, Nigel. It smells off to me, and you're racing tomorrow.'

As Nigel bent forward to smell the cream, Way pushed his face deep into the dish. Mansell went to the washroom to clean up, and when David joined him Mansell sprayed water all over the front of his trousers.

That was not sweet enough revenge for Mansell. At the next race-meeting banquet in Nottingham, he quietly tipped a waiter £20 to put a huge dish of cream on one side. He then told the waiter to ask David Way if he would like extra cream on his dessert. When he replied that he would, Nigel nipped out and got the dish and tipped the entire contents over David's head.

This sparked a free-for-all, with soda syphons the favourite weapons. Colin Chapman pretended to try to push Nigel out of a window, and took the opportunity to shove a cream cake in the pocket of Nigel's cashmere jacket. Who said that Nigel Mansell was dull?

KEITH FLETCHER, the king of Essex cricket who became captain and then manager of England, has a reputation for being somewhat absent-minded. This was no better illustrated than when he was introducing his England players to Prime Minister Mrs Gandhi during the 1981 tour of India when he was skipper. As Fletch reached Surrey wicket-keeper Jack Richards in the presenation line-up he had one of his blank moments. 'This, ma'am, is um, er ...' He then whispered to a startled Richards, 'C'mon, mate. Help me out. I've forgotten ... what's your ruddy name?'

Further down the line, Fletch introduced Lancashire bowler Paul Allott as John Arlott.

Last word in this chapter goes to one of the greatest characters of them all, **IAN BOTHAM**. Playing for England against Australia in Brisbane on the 1982-83 tour, Both was struggling to break down the resistance of century-maker Kepler Wessels. He said to Allan Lamb – like Wessels – born and raised in South Africa: 'You must know a few Afrikaans swear words. Have a go at him.'

2: Just Amazing

This is a gathering of curious, odd and downright bizarre sports stories that defy belief. They are, in fact, Just Amazing ...

Helen Stephens and Stanislawa Walasiewicz dominated women's sprinting during the 1930s. Miss Walasiewicz, born in Poland but raised in the United States, was Olympic 100 metres champion in 1932, and took the silver behind Miss Stephens in the 1936 Berlin Olympics. Miss Stephens was accused by Polish officials of being more man than woman, and she took a sex test to disprove the allegation. She retired with an unbeaten sprint record, while her arch rival Miss Walasiewicz – who changed her name to Stella Walsh – continued her career during which she set eleven world records and won forty-one USA sprint championships. On December 4, 1980 – forty years after hanging up her spikes – Miss Walsh was out shopping at a Cleveland store when she was innocently caught in the cross-fire during a robbery attempt. She was shot dead. An autopsy revealed that the athletics heroine of the thirties had male sexual organs. The Polish officials had levelled their accusations at the wrong athlete.

Australian cricket ace Dennis Lillee was so furious when the umpires ruled that he could not use his revolutionary aluminium bat against England in the Perth Test against England in 1979 that he hurled it farther than he had been hitting the ball with the bat. In the second innings he scored 19 with a traditional willow before the headline-writers got the special wicket they had been waiting for: *'Lillee caught Willey bowled Dilley.'* Even more hilarious was this descriptive piece of commentary from Brian Johnston during Test Match Special: 'The bowler's Holding, the batsman's Willey.'

Brian, the much-mourned Voice of Cricket and one of the funniest of all raconteurs, told me this cracker during one of his numerous visits to the *This Is Your Life* studio: 'Frank Tyson was going through the Australian batsmen like a dose of salts on the famous tour Down Under during which he bowled as fast as any man had ever bowled. It was soon the turn of the Australian number 11 to come into bat. He nervously made his way down the pavilion steps and, looking anxious and apprehensive, he attempted to shut the wooden gate behind him but could not get the catch to connect. A nearby spectator filled him with confidence by shouting, '"Don't bother to close it. You won't be long."'

Ralph Walton was adjusting his gumshield as he left his corner for the start of a contest in Lewiston, Maine, in 1946. His opponent, Al Couture, raced across the ring and knocked him out with a swinging right to the jaw. The 'fight' was all over in a record 10.5 seconds, including the count. It was reported that Walton's second consoled him by telling him that he was ahead on points at the time.

Henry Armstrong, who held the featherweight, lightweight and welterweight titles at one and the same time, was shadow boxing in the gymnasium in preparation for a title fight in 1938 when he tripped on a torn canvas and knocked himself out. He slipped a disc in the fall and his contest had to be postponed.

Mike Gibbons was a clever boxer whose evasive now-you-see-me-now-you-don't tactics earned him the nickname 'the St Paul Phantom'. After he had outclassed a highly-rated opponent, Augie Ratner, over ten rounds in New York in 1923, Ratner said to his manager, 'In future match me with only one guy at a time.'

The British Open Golf championship committee tightened their entry rules after Maurice Flitcroft, a 46-year-old crane driver from Barrow-in-Furness, carded a record 121 strokes in the first qualifying round at Formby in Lancashire in 1976. 'I could have done with a bit more practice,' he said.

American professional golfer Harry Gonder set out to prove a theory that a scratch golfer should be able to land a hole in one in a given number of shots. He filled a bucket with balls and, with two local club officials in tow as witnesses, he went to the tee at the 160-yard third hole. He estimated that it would take no longer than half an hour for him to get an ace. He bombarded the flag with balls, and came within fifteen inches of the hole with his 86th shot. Harry took a break for lunch after failing to get the elusive hole in one with 941 shots. His 55th shot on his restart came to rest just three inches from the flag, but still no ace. He continued on right through the afternoon and long into the night, but finally had to concede defeat at three o'clock the next morning after playing for more than 16 hours and in the glare of car lights. Harry had played a total of 1,817 shots without getting a hole in one. Three months later, playing in competition, he holed out with a seven iron.

The baseball commentator at the Illinois radio station was working from a telegraph service, delivering his 'live' on-air descriptions from a downtown studio as he tore each report from the wire machine. There was a sudden break in transmission, and the commentator decided to ad-lib, creating for the listeners his imaginative version of what he thought was happening in the 1933 World Series. The next day's newspapers revealed that the action had been nowhere near where his mouth was. The commentator was a young actor called Ronald 'The Great Communicator' Reagan.

Baronet's son Vere Thomas St Leger Gould, lawn tennis champion of Ireland and runner-up at Wimbledon in 1879, later became involved in a grisly murder case. He was found guilty of murdering a Danish widow, and attempting to freight the dismembered body in two luggage trunks from the south of France to England in 1907. He died in a cell on Devil's Island where he was serving a life sentence.

Jack Bloomfield, British light-heavyweight champion, stepped up to the heavyweight division to fight Bombardier Billy Wells in 1922. After knocking out the veteran Wells in the sixth round, the sporting Bloomfield bent to pick up his stricken opponent and gave himself a hernia.

Californian James J. Corbett, the first gloved heavyweight champion of the world, was named after an uncle who was a priest in Ireland. He had hoped to follow his uncle as a priest, but this dream died when he was expelled from the Sacred Heart College for head-butting one of the college Brothers in the stomach as he attempted to cane the young Corbett.

Heavyweights André Anderson and Charles Weinert topped a boxing bill at the New York Opera House in 1916. According to the *New York Times* reporter, Weinert was counted out while trying to release himself from the mouth of a bass horn after being knocked out of the ring into the orchestra pit.

John Snow, Sussex and England fast bowler, came roaring in to bowl to Leicestershire batsman Paul Marner, who went on to his back foot to hook what was a loose false toss. As his bat connected, the 'ball' disintegrated. Snow and the rest of the Sussex team were on their knees in helpless laughter. Snow had bowled a bar of red soap. He said to the local newspaper reporter that it was the start of a clean-up-cricket campaign.

Alfred Knight, England and Leicestershire batsman in the early part of the century, was a Methodist lay preacher who used to kneel and pray in the dressing-room before going out to bat. He also occasionally used to kneel in front of the stumps and offer a prayer. He once went on one knee to pray while at the wicket during a County match against Lancashire. Walter Brearley, a fiery fast bowler of Freddie Trueman-type temperament, was preparing to bowl, and yelled, 'Owzat!' The umpire asked, 'On what ground?' Walter pointed down the wicket at the praying Knight and said, 'On the grounds that he's getting unfair assistance from above.'

Australian captain Greg Chappell ordered his brother Trevor to bowl the last ball of a one-day international underarm so that tailend New Zealand batsman Brian McKechnie had no chance of hitting a match-winning boundary. It was within the laws, but brought world-wide condemnation from cricket lovers. In New Zealand a mock advertisement was drawn up for a new underarm deodorant. The headline read, 'It's Chappell, and it really stinks'.

Glamorgan's County match against Gloucestershire at Ebbw Vale in 1948 was held up when a flock of sheep wandered on to the ground. Nine months earlier, a game between South Australia and Queensland was stopped by a plague of thousands of grasshoppers hopping over the pitch. A swarm of bees held up play during Oxford University's match against Worcestershire at The Parks in 1962.

Garrincha, the Brazilian wing genius who won World Cup winners' medals in 1958 and 1962, had two left feet. Both his feet were shaped the same way and he wore two left boots. He was a country boy nicknamed Little Bird, and he kept more than seventy pet birds at his village home.

The night that Ipswich Town clinched the League championship in 1962, manager Alf Ramsey did a solo lap of honour round the Portman Road pitch in a deserted stadium, with only chairman John Cobbold as a witness.

Scot Archie Hunter was one of Aston Villa's first great captains at the turn of the century. He was so important to the team that when he was unable to travel with the official party to a match against Notts County a special train was hired to take him to Nottingham.

Arsenal were in danger of going bankrupt soon after gaining admission to the Second Division in 1893. They were the only team south of Birmingham, and the travelling costs were crippling them. They got themselves out of trouble by organising an archery tournament that raised a life-saving £1,200.

Nottingham Forest penalty expert Harry Martin was lying

in the dressing-room being treated for an injury when Forest were awarded a spot-kick against Bolton on Boxing Day, 1924. He was carried from the dressing-room to take the vital kick, scored and then collapsed again and was carried back to the dressing-room.

Jack Fairbrother, Newcastle United's goalkeeper when they won the FA Cup in 1951, once mislaid his gloves before a game and borrowed a pair from a friendly policeman patrolling behind the goal. Newcastle won the match, and from then on superstition demanded that he always wore policemen's white gloves. He became a regular visitor to Market Street police station in Newcastle where they were only too pleased to give him a helping hand.

Jump jockey Simon Mills was thrown by his mount, Sir Sagamore, in a chase at Adelaide in 1992. His foot became caught in the stirrup and he was dragged along the ground all the way to the next fence. As he was trying to unhook his foot, Sir Sagamore took off and horse and jockey cleared the fence. His foot was released as he landed, and Mills escaped with a broken arm and loosened teeth. 'I am convinced the horse knew he had to leap higher than ever before in his life to make sure I cleared that fence,' said Mills.

National Hunt jockey Graham Thorner was clearing a fence when his breeches split. The jockeys following him were in danger of falling out of their saddles with laughter at the sight of his bare, jock-strapped bottom popping out.

Martin Gibbs, a leading National Hunt rider in the first quarter of the century, shrugged when he was told that whips and spurs would not be allowed at a point-to-point meeting in the Midlands. He craftily inserted tin tacks into his riding boots.

One of the more unusual races was staged at Huntingdon in 1763. A man ran against a racehorse over two furlongs, with 100 guineas as the prize. The horse was handicapped by having one leg strapped. The race was awarded to the man when the strapping on the horse came undone.

Ted 'Kid' Lewis, Britain's former world welterweight champion, fought American Jack Britton 20 times over a period of six years between 1915 and 1921. Lewis won three bouts, Britton four, one was drawn and there were twelve 'no decision' contests. They often lost their purses to each other in card games in the dressing-room before the fights. An Australian fighter who borrowed Kid Lewis's name was involved in a bizarre contest in Australia in 1968. His opponent, Dimitri Michael, had an angry disagreement with his cornerman at the end of the first round. The second whipped his stool away and took it with him as he left the ringside. Michael found no stool and no second when he got back to the corner at the end of the second round. The referee ruled the fight 'no contest'.

Referee Tommy Little held up the hand of Tongan Johnny Halafihi to signify that he was the points winner at the end of the tenth round of his Commonwealth title fight eliminator against South African Mike Holt at Nottingham Ice Rink in 1960. It was pointed out to Little that it was a 12-round contest. Two rounds later he declared a draw.

More than 1,000 spectators in New York paid to watch two boxers miming to the action of the world heavyweight title fight return between Gene Tunney and Jack Dempsey in

Chicago. A round-by-round report of the contest was telegraphed to New York and the look-alike boxers acted out the action to a ringside commentary

When rivals Bob Fitzsimmons and Peter Maher arrived in Langtry, Texas, for a $10,000 sidestake fight in 1892 they found a posse of Texas Rangers waiting with orders to stop them fighting because boxing was banned in the State. However, Judge Roy Bean, a friend of the promoter and a fight fan, and the most famous law enforcer in Texas, came up with a novel solution to save the contest. While all the fighters' connections adjourned to the Jersey Lily Saloon – owned by Judge Bean – a team of hired hands erected a ring just across the border in Mexico. The boxers, the fight officials and more than two hundred supporters then walked over a pontoon bridge that had been thrown across the Rio Grande. Bat Masterton, the famed marshal of Dodge City and a boxing fanatic, stood at the entrance of the tent with six-shooters drawn to discourage any would-be troublemakers. The fight lasted just over a minute. Fitzsimmons sidestepped a left lead from Maher, and then threw a right counter that landed flush on the jaw and stretched the Irishman out on the canvas. It was the only contest on the bill. Never in sporting history had so much trouble been taken for such little action.

Italian deaf-mute Mario D'Agta was world bantamweight boxing champion in the 1950s. Ringposts were fitted with electric lights so that he knew when a round had finished.

In the third round of his title defence against French challenger Alphonse Halimi in Paris on April Fool's Day, 1957, the lights above the ring exploded. Flaming debris fell on D'Agata's shoulders. He insisted on fighting on after treatment, and was beaten on points over 15 rounds.

World middleweight champion Stanley Ketchel, the 'Michigan Assassin', challenged Jack Johnson for the world heavyweight title at Colma, California, in 1909. The two boxers struck a private agreement that Ketchel would be allowed to go the distance for the benefit of the movie cameras, because a short-lived fight would not have been a draw at the cinemas. But Ketchel forgot the deal and briefly (and unwisely) floored Johnson with a sneak punch in the twelfth round. Seconds later Ketchel had two of his teeth embedded in Johnson's right glove after being knocked cold. Johnson hit him so hard that the champion fell over as he landed his devastating final punch.

Dinny Pails, the Australian who was number one seed for the men's Wimbledon singles title in 1946, got lost on the London Underground on the way to Wimbledon for his quarter-final against Yvon Petra. He arrived twenty minutes late to find Queen Mary was among the spectators he had kept waiting. His nerve went and he was beaten in four sets by Petra, who gave the credit for his success to a German prison camp surgeon. Petra, a Frenchman born in Indo-China, was seriously wounded during the war and taken prisoner by the Nazis. He was told that his leg would have to be amputated, but it was saved by the skill of the surgeon.

Czechoslovakia lost their Davis Cup tie against Yugoslavia in Zagreb in 1938 by default after Franz Cejnar failed to reappear following a break for bad light during his final deciding match. Cejnar was later discovered trying to climb out of the dressing-room window. Somebody had locked him in and the key was missing.

Tony Fawcett, of Zimbabwe, and Britain's Keith Class got locked in one of the longest games on record in the first round of the Surrey championships at Surbiton in 1975. It lasted 31 minutes and they contested 37 deuces and 80 points in all.

Bob Burrows, a fast bowler with Worcestershire in the first quarter of the century, was known as a destroyer of stumps. It got to the point where they started measuring how far the bails flew when he hit the target. When he bowled Lancashire's great Archie MacLaren at Old Trafford in 1901 one of the bails was found down by the boundary 64 yards 6 inches away. Burrows beat this record when bowling at Old Trafford ten years later. This time Bill Huddleston was his victim, and one of the bails actually reached the boundary 67 yards 6 inches away.

Batsman David Pritchard was walking from the pavilion to the middle to start his innings in a charity match when the '0' plate on the scoreboard was caught by the wind. It flew off and hit him on the head.

Southgate cricketer John MacIldowie must have wondered what sort of a match he was in for when he dropped a dolly catch in the opening overs of a club game against Barnet. He made amends by taking all ten Barnet wickets for 22 runs, and he hit the stumps every time.

This is not a shaggy dog story: Northants wicket-keeper

Keith Andrew was credited with a four when his shot against Hampshire at Southampton was picked up inside the boundary ropes by a stray dog ... and Sussex batsman Ian Thomson was awarded a four after his shot against the West Indies tourists was fielded by a dog before the ball had reached the boundary.

Glamorgan tail-ender Peter Judge has the dubious distinction of being the only batsman in first class cricket to have been bowled for two first-ball ducks in successive balls and in the same match. He was last man out against the Indian tourists in 1946 when he was bowled first ball by leg spinner Chandra Sarwate. India enforced the follow-on and as time was running out, the Glamorgan skipper signalled to Judge to stay out in the middle to start the next innings. Sarwate was again the bowler and clean bowled him with the first ball.

Derek Pringle, Essex and England bowler, once pulled out of a Test match because he had damaged his back while writing a letter.

Alan Mullery, former Tottenham and Fulham captain, once pulled out of an England tour because he had damaged his back while shaving.

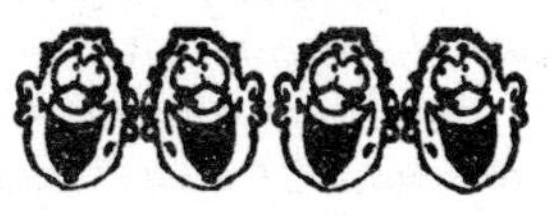

Derek Ibbotson failed to qualify for the 1957 AAA finals when he could not win his heat against undistinguished opposition. A week later at London's White City the Yorkshireman broke the world mile record with a run of 3mins. 57.2secs.

Ron Hill, former European and Commonwealth marathon champion, has not missed a single day's running on the road since 1964. He calculates that he has been on the run for more than 10,000 consecutive days, and he has competed in a record 53 countries.

Jewey Smith was sitting in his dressing-room in Paris waiting for his welterweight contest against New Yorker Willie Lewis, whom he had never even seen, when an American tourist invited himself in. He was wearing full evening dress, a cloak and carrying an opera hat. 'I've just called in to commiserate with you,' said the tourist. 'What are you talking about?' asked Lewis. 'Well,' said the tourist, 'the man you are meeting tonight is the finest boxer I have ever seen and I'm afraid he will be giving you a good hiding.' At that moment Smith's manager came in, and ordered out the tourist. He just happened to be Willie Lewis, the man who invented the Ali-style taunting of opponents. He stopped Smith in the tenth round.

Gerardo Martinez literally came unstuck when he slipped and stumbled to defeat against Raul Perez, who won the WBC world bantamweight championship in 1988. The manager of Martinez came up with a unique excuse. He claimed that his boxer's boots had been got at, and that somebody had sprayed grease on the soles to stop him getting a foothold. An independent laboratory report confirmed that the boots had been smeared with a greasy substance.

Just before the first bell rang at the start of Jack Dempsey's world heavyweight title challenge against Jess Willard, his manager Doc Kearns told him that he had bet his entire purse that he would win in the first round. Dempsey floored the giant Willard seven times in the first three minutes and left the ring thinking he was the champion after the referee had counted out Willard. But the time-keeper revealed that the bell had gone to end the first round before he had finished the count. Dempsey was summoned back to finish the demolition, eventually winning in the third round. He had won the title but lost his purse. It was alleged that his hand bandages had been soaked in plaster of Paris before the fight. 'Oh no they were not,' said his manager Doc Kearns. 'We used cement!'

Transfer-seeking goalkeeper Peter Shilton once got into trouble with the Leicester City directors for making a

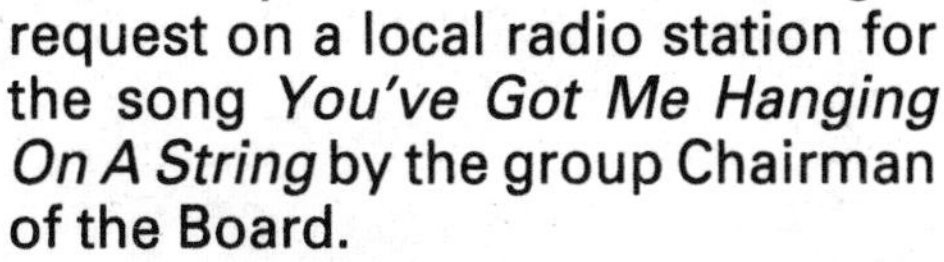

request on a local radio station for the song *You've Got Me Hanging On A String* by the group Chairman of the Board.

I scripted the *This Is Your Life* tribute to Shilts, and one of the facts we uncovered was that when he was a boy he used to hang for hours from the banisters at home to stretch his arms.

John Burridge, one of the most experienced goalkeepers in the British game, idolised Shilton to the extent that he took a photograph of him to the hair-dresser's.

He showed the photo to the hair-dresser, and said, 'Give me a Peter Shilton.'

When Burridge first turned professional he was told by a trainer, 'All goalkeeper are crazy, and you fit the bill perfectly.' Joker Burridge said it was one of the nicest things anybody had ever said to him!

Bill 'Fatty' Foulke was the heaviest man ever to play for

England. The Sheffield United goalkeeper weighed anything between 18 and 22 stone, according to how his appetite was at the time. He was slow to get down to low shots, but perfected booted clearances. He had a volatile temper, and playing against Liverpool at Anfield in 1898 the man mountain erupted when Liverpool's star forward George Allan shoulder-charged him. He picked Allan up by the ankles, stood him on his head in the mud and bounced him up and down. Foulke's career ended sadly when, flat broke, he earned a living on Blackpool Beach by inviting holidaymakers to try to beat him from 12 yards at a 'alfpenny a shot.

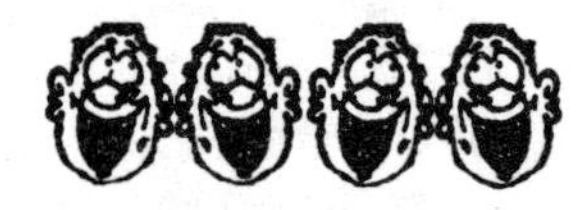

England bowler Gubby Allen, later to become the game's number one administrator, included four no balls and three wides in his 13-ball first over against Australia at Old Trafford in 1934. Warwickshire fast bowler Gladstone Small surpassed this at Coventry when he bowled 11 no balls and a wide in an 18-ball over against Middlesex in 1982.

Arthur Dolphin, Yorkshire and England batsman, was in the Lord's pavilion preparing to bat against Middlesex. He reached for a pad, lost his balance, and fell off his chair and broke his wrist.

Ian Greig got a crack on the hand while captaining Surrey against the Pakistan tourists in 1987. An X-ray hospital revealed a fractured finger. As he prepared to leave the X-ray room he banged his head on the machine and had to have three stitches inserted in a cut on his head.

Yorkshire master Wilfred Rhodes was all set to acknowledge a double century against Sussex at Hove in 1909 when the umpire ruled that his partner had fallen short with one of his runs. Rhodes was bowled with the next ball for 199.

The good news for that elegant stylist Tom Graveney was that he scored 200 runs for Gloucestershire against Glamorgan at Newport in 1956. The bad news: Gloucestershire were all out for 298.

The bad news for Yorkshire and England batting master Len Hutton was that he collected three successive ducks in June, 1949. The even worse news for bowlers: it briefly interrupted a one-man assault during which Hutton gathered 1,294 runs during that blazing month of June.

Oxford University batsman Gerald Crutchley retired at 99 not out against Cambridge University in 1912 ... suffering from measles.

Arthur Denton lost a leg during the First World War, but he continued to bat for Northamptonshire with the aid of a runner.

Hugh 'Toey' Tayfield, South African slow bowler, delivered 137 consecutive balls in a Test match against England in 1957 without conceding a single run.

South African Gerry Brand dropped a goal against England at Twickenham in 1932 from just in front of the Springbok posts. The ball was estimated to have travelled 90 yards before going through the England posts.

New Zealand Rugby coach Eric Watson introduced an unusual training method for the 1980 All Blacks tourists.

He was so concerned at how many passes were going astray that he made the three-quarters practise their running movements while using a house brick instead of a ball. The press dubbed them the 'All Bricks'.

Tony O'Reilly, billionaire head of Heinz, was recalled for his final Ireland Rugby international cap against England at the age of 34 in 1971. He arrived at Twickenham in a chauffeur-driven Rolls-Royce. Skipper Willie John McBride took him on one side and said, 'Tony, you won't mind me saying to your face that you that you're no longer in your prime. The tactic I suggest you adopt is shake your jowls at your opposite number.'

Dickie Bird, the most popular of all umpires, was standing in the middle during a match at Northampton when Allan Lamb came into bat. He handed him a mobile telephone, saying, 'Look after this for me, please, Dickie. I didn't want to leave it in the dressing-room.' Five minutes later the telephone rang. Dickie took it out of his pocket and answered it. Ian Botham was on the line asking him the score.

A cricketer who could match even Botham and Lamb as a prankster was former Hampshire skipper Colin Ingleby-Mackenzie, whose cavalier approach to the game (and life) is best summed up by his famous quote, 'I always insist that my players are in bed before ten o'clock during a match. After all, play starts at 11.30.' During his playing days with Yorkshire, Dickie Bird was shaping up to face a ball against Hampshire at Bournemouth when he heard the sound of a radio horse race commentary. He looked towards the slips to find Ingleby-Mackenzie with a transistor to his ear. 'Hope I'm not breaking your concentration, old chap,' said Ingers. 'I've got a few bob riding on a nag.'

A spectator hit by two successive sixes by Yorkshire's Steven Rhodes at Scarborough in 1990 was offered the use of a helmet by one of the fielders.

Worcestershire leg spinner Roly Jenkins completed two hat-tricks in the same match against Surrey in 1949.

The famous racing cry 'They're off!' was heard so many times at the 1863 Derby that when the field did finally get off few really believed it. There were no fewer than thirty-four false starts, many of them caused by rank outsider Tambour Major, who was finally left behind. George Fordham, riding the favourite, was beaten by a neck. On his way back to the unsaddling enclosure Fordham – nicknamed 'The Demon' – overheard a spectator say that he had thrown the race. He leapt off his horse, grabbed hold of the punter and hurled him into a bed of prickles.

There has never been a Derby quite like that of 1846, when the leading jockey coming off Tattenham Corner was drunk. The gentleman in the saddle was William Scott, one of the outstanding jockeys of his time and a younger brother of John Scott, the 'Wizard of the North' trainer. Scott was riding Sir Tatton Sykes, which he also owned. He rode it to victory in the 2,000 Guineas, and it was highly fancied for the Derby. But as Scott stood at the Epsom bar getting steadily sloshed, the odds of his horse drifted until it had gone out to 16-1. He had to be helped into the saddle, and was so engrossed in a slanging match with the starter that he didn't see the flag fall and was left several lengths behind the field. Scott stormed after his departing rivals, still shouting abuse over his shoulder at the starter. He had made up the lost ground going into Tattenham Corner and was in a commanding lead with two furlongs to go. But Scott, a puppet of alcohol, lurched in his saddle and started taking a diagonal course towards the stand. Sam Day drove the chestnut Pyrrhus the First through on the inside to win by a neck. It's a sobering thought that Scott might have helped Sir Tatton Sykes become the first horse to win the Triple Crown. He piloted it to victory in the St Leger three months later, and his only drinking was done in celebration.

Jess Willard, the giant Kansas cowboy who took the world heavyweight title from Jack Johnson, boxed a trial early in his career with a vaudeville strong man calling himself 'The Great Romanos'. He was told that if he could handle himself well he would be launched as a 'white hope' ahead of Willard. A couple of rights from Willard took the legs away from the travelling man, and the promoters lost interest in 'The Great Romanos', who had once gone the distance in a non-title fight against Jack Johnson. He left the Midwest and headed for California, ending up in Hollywood where he won an Academy Award for Best Actor in *The Informer* in 1935. His real name was Victor McLaglen, and he was a British-born actor who became an established movie star.

Jack Munroe, a Canadian miner and former footballer, was knocked out in two rounds in a 1904 fight against world heavyweight title contender James J. Jeffries. Munroe left the ring with chants of 'coward' ringing in his ears because he had shown little stomach for the fight. Eleven years later he won Canada's highest military honour for his heroism during fighting in the trenches in the First World War. Ignoring his own wounds, he dragged a crippled officer to safety while chopping down enemy soldiers with his favourite weapon, a woodsman's axe. Nobody ever called him a coward again.

The elderly man sat in the back of a cab at a red light in midtown Manhattan when two muggers opened the doors and demanded money. 'Let me get out and I'll see what I've got for you,' he said. What he had for them was two punches. He flattened one mugger with a left hook and the other with a right to the jaw. He then climbed back into the cab and told the driver to continue the journey. His destination was the famous restaurant he owned in New York – Jack Dempsey's. The muggers had picked on 'The Manassa Mauler', arguably the hardest heavyweight puncher of all time. Jack regaled his customers with the story of how he had dealt with the muggers. They would not have disputed his claim that 'the last thing that a fighter loses is his punch.'

Primo Carnera was a newcomer to the United States at the start of his build-up as a challenger for the world heavyweight championship. The Italian man mountain, dubbed 'The Ambling Alp', was asked on his arrival in California what he thought of Los Angeles. 'Los Angeles?' said Primo. 'I knocka hima outta in two rounds.'

Big, bad Sonny Liston was hardly famous for his sense of fun, but there was one time when he was seen laughing uncontrollably. During a world title press conference the subject somehow got round to whether white men or black men have most hair on their legs. Sonny, a notorious gambler, announced, 'I'll bet any white man in this room $50 that I've got less hair on my legs than him.' Reg

Gutteridge, ITV's Voice of Boxing, couldn't resist it and took the bet. He rolled up his trousers to show a completely hairless false leg. Reg had had a leg blown off when he stepped on a mine during the D-Day landings. Sonny paid up as he almost fell off his chair laughing. Sonny, 'Old Stoneface', had his own eccentric brand of humour which is best captured in the story of when, just before giving a television interview, he staged a mock row with a colleague over a $100 loan. Suddenly Liston pulled a revolver and shot his friend, who collapsed with blood seeping from his chest. The bullet was a blank and the blood was red sauce, but it was realistic enough to cause one of the television crew to faint.

Jack Roper, knocked out in one round during Joe Louis's 'Bum A Month' campaign, talked a great fight before the first bell rang and told reporters how he was going to pound Louis to defeat. Asked what had gone wrong with his plans, he said: 'I zigged when I shoulda zagged.'

Newcastle United missed a first-minute penalty against Newport County in a Second Division match at St James' Park in 1946. That was the bad news. The good news for Geordie fans is that they went on to win 13-0! Len Shackleton, making his debut after a transfer from Bradford Park Avenue for £13,000, scored six goals. 'I think I'd better hang up my boots now,' said Shack.

George Best set a have-boots-will-travel record in 1977 when in a period of just 10 days he played in all four home countries. He represented Northern Ireland against Iceland in Belfast, and then played club matches for Fulham against Cardiff in Wales, against St Mirren in Scotland and, finally, he faced Crystal Palace at Selhurst Park.

Alan Ball scored inside the first minute for Arsenal against West Ham at Highbury in 1972. Four years later Ball gave a carbon-copy performance when he scored inside the first minute for Arsenal against West Ham at Highbury.

The BBC newsreader wondered if somebody was playing a joke on him when he was handed the First Division results to announce on the afternoon of Boxing Day 1963. There were ten games played, and this is how they finished:

Blackpool 1, Chelsea 5
Burnley 6, Manchester United 1
Fulham 10, Ipswich Town 1
Leicester City 2, Everton 0
Liverpool 6, Stoke City 1
Nottingham Forest 3, Sheffield United 3
Sheffield Wednesday 3, Bolton Wanderers 0
West Bromwich Albion 4, Tottenham Hotspur 4
West Ham United 2, Blackburn Rovers 8
Wolves 3, Aston Villa 3

It is remembered as the day that football went Christmas crackers. There were 66 goals scored in the ten matches and three players – Graham Leggat (Fulham), Andy Lochead (Burnley), and Roger Hunt (Liverpool) – helped themselves to four goals each. The craziest game was at Craven Cottage where Ipswich took a ten-goal hammering against a Fulham side that had England internationals Johnny Haynes, Alan Mullery, George Cohen and a stylish, upright midfield player called Bobby Robson in no mood to show Christmas charity. But it was a Scot – international centre-forward Graham Leggat – who did most to make the Ipswich defenders look like a gathering of repentant Scrooges determined to give everything away for Christmas. He scored four times and could easily have doubled his score during a match in which Fulham were made to look like world beaters. Yet Ipswich, League champions the previous year, managed to laugh away the heaviest defeat in their history. The late and much-liked John Cobbold, then their chairman, said afterwards with typical wit, 'Our problem was our goalkeeper was sober. The rest of us, myself included, were still nursing Christmas Day hangovers.'

King George V once got himself locked in the lavatory during a finals day visit to Wimbledon. Mrs Rosie Cherry, in charge of one of the women's dressing-rooms, heard his distress call and crashed the door open with her shoulder.

American tennis coach Bill White claimed an unusual record while giving a lesson at the Merion Club, Philadelphia, in 1930. He held thirteen balls in one hand while serving.

In the 1927 final of the Cannes lawn tennis championship, Henri Cochet beat Jacques Brugnon 1-6, 6-1, 6-0, 1-6, 6-0, probably the least number of games contested in a five-set championship final.

Willie Renshaw, one of the early kings of the Wimbledon courts, made the most astonishing comeback in the history of the tournament against Harry Barlow in 1889. Having already saved six match points, Willie trailed 0-5 in the final set. He battled back to level the scorers and finally ran out the winner 8-6. Willie then met his twin brother Ernest in the Challenge Round final and won in four sets for a record seventh Wimbledon singles title.

Ilie Nastase was the clown prince of the Wimbledon courts, but his humour often boiled over into anger as he became embroiled in disputes with umpires and line judges. One of his most publicised clashes came with a very English Wimbledon umpire, who infuriated the Romanian by calling him Nastase. 'It's Mr Nastase,' said Illie. The umpires considered this, and then said: 'Look here, Nastase, we used to have a famous cricket match in this country called Gentlemen versus Players. The Gentlemen were put down on the scorecard as "Mister" because they were gentlemen. By no stretch of the imagination can anybody call you a gentleman.'

Brian Barnes, one of the favourite characters on the European golf circuit, was lining up a putt on the green during the Italian Open watched by a 'gallery' consisting of a single spectator. The one observer was standing in Brian's eye line and he asked him to move. But the spectator stood his ground. Finally, in frustration, Brian summoned a tournament official and asked him to get the spectator to move. The Italian official went to the man in the gallery and after some animated conversation returned to report in a heavy accent, 'He says thata as he paida to come in to watcha he can standa wherea he likesa. He says thata if youa do notta like it, you will havea to movea your balla.'

Jesper Parnevik, one of the swarm of Swedish golfers making an impact on the European circuit, was so angry with himself over a round he played at St Merion that he dived into the duck pond alongside the eighteenth green. His temper is controlled compared to that of his countryman Anders Forsbrand. He has been seen attacking greens with his club after missed putts, and several clubs have been snapped over his knee. Tony Johnstone, of Zimbabwe, can also let fly, and in a temper he once snapped a golf club, which was put into a bin in the locker room. Mark Roe, the 1994 winner of the French Open, fished out the club and had it mounted on a board for special presentation ceremony. Roe is a Jekyll and Hyde on the course. He is the joker who once arrived on the first tee wearing a Captain Hook mask, but he can also be fiery. He once threw a club into the bushes after a poor shot, and it took him and his caddie three minutes to find it. Concerned about the threat of fines for swearing, Roe said: 'I've trained myself to mutter a special substitute cuss word of my own. Rather than risk getting a fine, I shout "Sheep-dip!"'

Detroit golfer Edward Ferguson played non-stop golf for 158 hours, hitting 3,999 shots while playing 828 holes and walking 327 miles. His score included a hole in one and an eagle, and his average for each rounds of 18 holes was 87.

At golf courses in Arizona you will find an added local rule: 'If your ball comes to rest within a club's length of a rattlesnake you are allowed to move it (the ball that is).'

And finally in this chapter of Just Amazing incidents, here are 12 novel ways that batsmen have found to get out...

Tailender James Southerton, who played for three different counties in one season, insisted he was out during a County match at The Oval in 1870 and walked off despite the umpire trying to call him back. It went into the scorebook as, 'J. Southerton, retired thinking he was out.'

Harold Heygate, of Sussex, was 'timed out' when he failed to reach the crease within the statutory two minutes after a fall of a wicket in the Sussex v Somerset County match at Taunton in 1918. He suffered from rheumatism and was unable to walk quickly enough to the wicket.

Leicestershire wicket-keeper Thomas Sidwell was one not out overnight against Surrey at The Oval in 1921. Making his way to the ground the next morning he managed to get himself lost on the London Underground. He arrived too late to bat, and it went down in the scorebook as 'absent, lost on tube'.

New Zealander Martin Donnelly, playing for Worcestershire, was hit on a foot by a ball from Middlesex spinner Jack Young in 1948. The ball looped in the air over Young's head, landed two feet behind the stumps and then spun back and hit the wicket.

Tom Pugh, a former Gloucestershire captain, ducked to avoid a bouncer which never got up and the ball hit him in the face, fracturing his jaw. He was given out lbw.

A ball from Athol Rowan ballooned up off the glove of Len Hutton during the fifth Test between England and South Africa at The Oval in 1951. As wicket-keeper Russell Endean reached for the ball, Hutton fended it away from the stumps with his bat and was given out for obstructing the field.

Non-striker Andrew Hilditch retrieved a wayward return and handed the ball to Sarfraz Nawaz during an Australia-Pakistan Test in 1979. Sarfraz appealed and Hilditch was given out 'handled ball'.

Former Warwickshire and England batsman Mike Smith

was facing a ball in a County match against Hampshire at Edgbaston in 1962 when a sudden gust of wind whipped his cap off his head. It fell on to the stumps and he was given out 'hit wicket'.

Close fielder Allan Lamb jumped to avoid a crashing shot from Wayne Phillips off the bowling of Phil Edmonds in the England-Australia Test at Edgbaston in 1985. The ball rebounded off Lamb's boot to be caught by David Gower.

A bouncer from Curtly Ambrose ricocheted off the jaw of Geoff Lawson and into the stumps during the Australia-West Indies Test at Perth in 1988. The umpire ruled 'retired hurt'.

Peter May, former Surrey and England skipper, was run out in peculiar circumstances while batting against Glamorgan at The Oval in 1957. He played uppishly towards wide mid-on, set off on a run and then saw Glamorgan fielder Bernard Hedges running in to take the catch. May took it that he had been caught and slowed to a walk. It was all happening behind his back. Hedges had dropped the catch, but then – with May on his lonely way back to the pavilion – lobbed the ball to the wicket-keeper. Glamorgan skipper Wilfred Wooller took the ball and broke the stumps.

Keith Miller, charismatic Australian all-rounder, was a journalist colleague of mine during our days together as sportswriters on the *Daily Express*. He told me this story of how his unusual dismissal when playing against England in the Headingley Test during the barnstorming 1948 tour: 'Young Neil Harvey was making his debut at the other end I decided to try to keep him from the strike while he settled in. I really went for the English bowling, and recall one six off Jim Laker hitting a pretty blonde girl in the crowd. I offered to go to her assistance, but the St John's ambulancemen beat me to it! Anyway, Harvey soon proved he needed no help from me as he helped himself to a magnificent century in 177 minutes. I attempted to keep pace with Neil and set my sights on a six off the bowling of Norman Yardley. He guessed my intentions and bowled the ball wide outside leg stump. I took a swing, overbalanced and the ball hit the bottom edge of my bat. It spun back behind me, whacked Godfrey Evans on the bonce and was spectacularly caught by Bill Edrich, who flung himself full length at first slip to hold the ball. I went back to the pavilion laughing my head off.'

3: Games for a Laugh

The Olympics provide the greatest sports show on earth. They are also often the Games for a Laugh. Here is a selection of the stranger moments, and also a look at some of the more extraordinary summer Olympic champions.

● James Connolly, the first champion at the revived Olympics in Athens in 1896, surrendered his place at Harvard to compete. The dean of Harvard had turned down his request to travel to Greece for the Games, so the head-strong student dropped out as, not for the last time, studies came second to the Olympic dream. Connolly, who later became a celebrated war correspondent, triple jumped to the first championship of the modern Olympics. He hopped, hopped again and then jumped to victory. He would have been disqualified at later Olympics because the correct sequence is a hop, *step* and a jump.

● A student at Princeton University, shot-put specialist Robert Garrett had heard of a discus but had never seen one before. While studying the Olympic programme before leaving for the 1896 Games in Athens, he noticed that the discus was one of the field events. Garrett asked a colleague what a discus looked like and was told it was one inch in thickness and twelve inches in width. He ordered one to be made, and when it arrived at Princeton it looked like a giant pancake and weighed nearly twenty pounds. He had half a dozen practice throws, and after nearly pulling his arm out of its socket decided to leave the discus to the Greeks. On arriving in Athens he was pleasantly surprised to find that a real discus was much smaller and lighter than the home-made implement he had been heaving about at Princeton. He entered the event at the last minute and surprised himself as much as his stylish Greek rivals by winning the championship with his final throw. He went on to win the shot and to take second place in the long jump and third place in the high jump.

● Defending his discus title in Paris in 1900, Garrett had a disastrous time. The competitors had to throw the discus in a straight line between an avenue of trees, taking care to miss the single large tree that was directly in line with the throwing circle. He kept bouncing the discus off the trees and was unplaced. The hammer-throwing competition took three times longer than expected because officials had to keep untangling the hammer wires from the surrounding trees. Irish-American strong-arm man John Flanagan collected the first of his three consecutive hammer-throwing titles.

● Britain's Launceston Elliott won the one-handed weight-lifting competition in the first of the modern Games in Athens in 1896 with a lift of just over 156 pounds. An attendant was unable to shift the weight with the use of two hands, and he looked on in embarrassment as Prince George, of Greece, picked it up with little trouble and tossed it to one side. The Prince was considered one of the strongest men in Greece, and many of his countrymen believe he would have won the competition had he entered.

● Rough seas caused the cancellation of the rowing and sailing programme in the 1896 Games, but the swimming went ahead as scheduled – in the open sea at Phaleron. There were waves of over ten feet, and the water was freezing. Three competitors had to be rescued from drowning, and dual Olympic champion Alfred (Guttman) Hajos, of Hungary, commented: 'My will to live completely overcame my desire to win.'

● Spyridon Louis, a former Greek shepherd and post-office messenger, won the first marathon of the modern Olympics, and was showered with gifts that made him comfortably well off for the rest of his life. The one prize he turned down was the offer of the hand of the daughter of millionaire Georgios Averoff, the chief benefactor of the Games. Louis was already a married man with two children.

● Michel Théato, a Parisian baker's delivery man, knew all the ins and outs and short-cuts of the back streets of Paris, and it was strongly suspected that he had used some of them on his way to victory in the marathon in the 1900 Paris Games. American Arthur Newton was convinced he had won the race. He claimed that he had taken the lead just after the halfway stage, and that nobody had overtaken him from then until the finish line. Newton, who had proved himself one of the world's great distance runners during the previous two years, could not believe it when he was told he had come in sixth, more than 30 minutes behind Théato. It was twelve years later that the Frenchman was officially confirmed as the winner.

● Another American, Dick Grant, brought an unsuccessful lawsuit against the Olympic International Committee. He claimed a cyclist had knocked him down as he was making a challenge for the lead in the 1900 Paris marathon. The race was poorly signposted, and there was no marshalling of the crowds of sightseers. Twelve of the nineteen starters gave up in a mixture of frustration and exhaustion, and several complained that they had got lost after getting wrong directions.

● Severe cramp forced Fred Lorz to drop out of the 1904 Olympic marathon in St Louis after nine miles, and he thumbed a lift to the stadium. The automobile in which he was travelling broke down and so Lorz completed the last four miles on foot. When he came trotting into the stadium far ahead of marathon leader Thomas Hicks, the crowd rose to acclaim Lorz, thinking he was the winner of the race. Lorz did nothing to disillusion them and allowed himself to be carried in triumph to the VIP area where he was introduced to Alice Roosevelt, the daughter of the President. He was about to be presented with the gold medal when officials who had been accompanying Hicks stopped the ceremony and exposed Lorz as an imposter. It was later announced that Lorz had been banned from athletics for life, but his explanation that he had only been playing a joke that got out of hand was accepted. He won the American marathon championship the following year without any motorised assistance. Hicks, representing the United States but born in Birmingham, was kept going over the final stages when – close to exhaustion – he was given liberal dosages of strychnine and brandy.

● Felix Carajal, a postman from Cuba, raised his boat fare to the United States for the 1904 St Louis Olympics by giving running exhibitions in the centre of Havana, and then taking a collecting bowl around the gathered crowds. During the boat trip to America he lost all his money in a dice game and had his athletics kitbag stolen. He hitched his way from the harbour of New Orleans to St Louis where he was entered in the marathon. He arrived two days later than planned, and on the very day of his event. Felix turned up for the start wearing shoes, long trousers and a long-sleeved shirt. American discus thrower Martin Sheridan felt sorry for him because everybody was laughing behind his back. He borrowed a pair of shears and trimmed his sleeves and trouser legs so that he at least looked like an athlete. Carvajal, running his first-ever marathon, was giving a good account of himself and was in with a medal chance when he came across a fruit orchard and started stuffing himself with apples and peaches. He then stood around chatting to spectators before returning to the race in which he delivered a late burst to finish a creditable fifth. Felix at least managed to avoid the experience of two South African competitors, who were chased three-quarters of a mile off course by a ferocious dog when contesting the lead.

● Dorando Pietri remains the most famous runner never to have won an Olympic marathon. The spindly-legged little candymaker from Capri was the first man into London's White City stadium after 26 miles in the 1908 Games. He then had 385 yards to go to reach the finishing line alongside the Royal box where Queen Alexander was waiting to greet the winner. It was a bridge too far. Dorando, in his white vest and knickerbockers and with a knotted handkerchief on his head, suddenly slowed to a drunken walk as he reached the cinder track. What should have been a lap of glory turned into a nightmare as he reeled on rubber legs, not knowing which way to turn for the finishing line. Doctors and officials crowded anxiously around him as the Italian crumpled slowly to the ground like a puppet that has had its strings cut. Four times he collapsed, and four times willing hands helped him up, finally guiding him through the tape. American John Hayes was second

across the line, finishing under his own steam. Dorando was disqualified for receiving assistance, and the gold medal went to Hayes. But it was Dorando who had captured the hearts of the British public, and Queen Alexandra was so moved by his performance that she presented him with a special gold cup. From that day on, the official distance of the marathon became 26 miles 385 yards. The 385 yards was the distance from the White City entrance to the Royal Box.

● American George Eyser, winner of two gold medals, two silvers and a bronze in the men's gymnastics at the 1904 St Louis Games, was one of the most remarkable Olympic champions of all. He had a wooden leg.

● London-Scot Wyndham Halswelle became the only man to win an Olympic medal unchallenged. He ran a solo lap in a re-run 400 metres final after his two American rivals had pulled out in protest at the disqualification of their team-mate John Carpenter. The first running of the final had been declared 'no race' after British officials ruled that Carpenter had run across Halswelle and blocked his run to the tape. Halswelle, a regular soldier who was a lieutenant in the British army, then went through the motions of running the race as he experienced the loneliness of the short-distance runner.

● Shot putter Ralph Rose, a 6ft 6in tall, 19-stone giant from California, used to breakfast on competition days on two pounds of steak, along with six eggs still in their shells! He was also well fed on success, winning the shot at the 1904 and 1908 Olympics, and taking the silver in 1912 in Stockholm where he was the gold medallist in the two-handed shot. Rose was also second in the discus and third in the hammer in the 1904 Games in St Louis. He volunteered to act as anchor man for the United States tug-of-war team in the 1908 London Games at the White City. He and his team-mates angrily pulled out of the competition after defeat against a British squad who, they claimed, were cheating by wearing illegal heavy boots that gave them a pulling advantage.

● Danish forward Sophus Nielsen helped himself to ten goals in a 17-1 thrashing of the French 'B' team in the early rounds of the 1908 Olympic football tournament. Four years later, Germany's Gottfried Fuchs repeated the ten-goal scoring feat against Russia. Great Britain, including the great Vivian Woodward, won the gold medals in 1908 and again in 1912. Represented by the Upton Park team, Great Britain were also winners of the first Olympic tournament in Paris in 1900.

● The fifth-placed competitor in the 1912 Olympic pentathlon was a 26-year-old American army lieutenant called George S. Patton. He surprised rivals in the shooting event by using a pearl-handled Colt revolver, the same weapon that he later always carried with him during World War Two as General 'Blood and Guts' Patton.

● Jim Thorpe, the Sac Indian from Oklahoma, whose tribal name was Wa-Tho-Huck, meaning Bright Path, was an extraordinary all-round sportsman. He once represented the Carlisle Indian School of Pennsylvania on his own in a meeting against a team from Lafayette College, and he won eight out of ten events. His strongest events were high jumping and high hurdling, and apart from winning the pentathlon and decathlon in Sweden in 1912, he also finished fourth in the individual high jump and seventh in the long jump. Six months after his phenomenal performance in the Games, the US Olympic Committee announced that they were ordering Thorpe to return his gold medals because they had evidence that he had played professional baseball. Thorpe's name was removed from the official records, with the runners-up being declared as substitute champions. It is true that Thorpe played in minor league professional baseball when little more than a schoolboy, but he had received only a few dollars' expenses. Following the disqualification scandal, he was forced to become a full-time professional sportsman and added to his record of renown with his feats on the American football field. In an *Associated Press* poll organised in the United States in 1950, Thorpe was voted the Athlete of the Half Century. Following his death in conditions of near poverty in 1953, the Indians commemorated their idol by erecting a monument in his memory. The town of Chunk, Pennsylvania, where he was buried changed its name to Jim Thorpe. His name was restored to the Olympic role of honour at a special ceremony in 1982, and his gold medals were presented to his children.

● In the same poll that Jim Thorpe was voted the Athlete of the Half Century, Mildred 'Babe' Didrikson was elected the greatest woman athlete. Not only did she win two gold medals and one silver in the 1932 Los Angeles Olympics, but during her amazing career she also hit three home runs in one baseball game, made an incredible 313 feet throw from the centre-field to the plate, was twice selected for the all-American basketball team, was an expert at diving, lacrosse and billiards, and was considered one of the greatest women golfers of all time. Born in 1914 in Port Arthur, Texas, of Norwegian parents, she first came to world prominence as a sixteen-year-old schoolgirl when she set a women's world record for the javelin. Shortly before the 1932 Olympics, she won the American national team athletic team championship on her own! The team that finished second had twenty-two competitors. In less than three hours she won five events and placed second in three more. Nicknamed 'Babe', she was the darling of the crowd at the Olympics in 1932 and gave them plenty to cheer by winning the final of the 80 metres hurdles in a world record 11.7 seconds. She also set a world record in winning the javelin with her very first throw, and was robbed of a possible third gold medal by a disputed disqualification in the high jump. She and her American team-mate Jean Shiley tied at a world record height. To decide the winner the bar was lowered a quarter of an inch to 5ft 5in for a jump-off. Shiley went clear and then Didrikson cleared the bar. The judges then announced they were disqualifying her because they considered her dive-dash-and-roll technique illegal. She had the consolation of being allowed to receive a silver medal. Banned from amateur athletics four months after the Games for using her name to promote automobile sales, Babe toured in a vaudeville act in which she gave exhibitions of her all-round sports skills and played the harmonica. In 1934 she switched to professional golf with astonishing success, winning all the major titles, including the women's world championship for four successive years. By then married to wrestler-showman George Zaharias, a twenty-stone man mountain known as the 'Crying Greek from Cripple Creek', she continued to tour the world as a golfer until a few months before her death from cancer in 1956.

● Greco-Roman middleweight wrestler Max Klein, of the Soviet Union, beat Finland's Alfred Asikainen in a 1912 final that lasted more than ten hours. They were said to be good friends at the end of the contest! Klein was too exhausted to take part in the final. The light-heavyweight final between Finland's Ivar Bohling and Swede Anders Ahlgren was declared a draw after a mere nine hours, and both men were presented with silver medals despite arguments that they should have each received a gold.

● There were seven false starts before the runners in the final of the men's 100 metres in the 1912 Olympics finally got away. The race was won by Ralph Craig, of the University of Michigan, who had been responsible for the first three breaks. In today's athletics he would have been disqualified after causing two false starts. Thirty-six years after his Olympic triumph, Craig was back in Olympic action with the United States yachting team in the 1948 London Games.

● Swedish long jumper William Peterssen was preparing to take his first jump in the 1920 Olympic final when he noticed a silver coin lying on the runway. He picked it up and found that it was an American quarter. Peterssen slipped it into his left shoe for good luck. The next jumper on the runway was American favourite Sol Butler, who pulled a muscle without registering a jump. Peterssen went on to a surprise victory.

● Sprinter Morris Kirksey, a member of the gold medal-winning USA relay team, finished the 1920 Games in a prison cell. He returned to his dressing-room to pick up his running shoes, only to find it locked. He was arrested as a suspected thief as he climbed through a window.

● There have been few more colourful characters in athletics than Italian walker Ugo Frigerio. While most walkers become tense and nervous when judges crouch alongside them to scrutinise their style, Frigerio used to engage them in conversation and thank them for their attention. He had a lot of talent to go with his warm personality, and won three Olympic gold medals. Just before the start of the 3,000-metre walk in the 1920 Antwerp Games he went to the bandleader in the middle of the field and handed him some sheet music. The band played his request during the race, and Frigerio walked in time to the music and conducted the crowd who responded with rhythmic clapping. He briefly stopped walking to signal to the bandleader to quicken the tempo and then went on to win the race by 20 metres.

● Philadelphia rower John B. Kelly created history in the 1920 Games when he became the first oarsman to win two sculling gold medals on the same day. Kelly, a bricklayer, had been barred from competing in the Diamond Sculls at Henley because the club he rowed for at home had been accused of professionalism, and also because he was a common bricklayer. He got his own back for this shameful treatment and stuck two oars up at the Henley snobs by beating Diamond Sculls winner Jack Beresford in the final. Kelly's daughter became Princess Grace of Monaco. Beresford was Britain's greatest oarsman before the emergence of Steve Redgrave, and collected three gold medals in five Olympiads.

● Host country Belgium were leading Czechoslovakia 2-0 in the football final in the 1920 Games in Antwerp when the Czechs walked off in a mass protest over a spate of controversial refereeing decisions. The Czechs, who had beaten the Belgians 15-1 in an earlier match, were disqualified and a play-off for second place was ordered between the losing semi-finalists. But France, who had been eliminated by the Czechs, refused to compete because several of their players had returned home, and eventually Spain defeated Holland for the silver medal.

● The Reverend Eric Liddell was Britain's champion and record holder over 100 yards, but he declined to take part in the Olympic 100 metres heats in the 1924 Games in Paris because they were to be staged on a Sunday, and it was against his strong religious principles. The never-on-Sunday sprinter, a Scottish rugby international, decided instead to compete in the 200 metres (he took the bronze medal), and, surprisingly, the 400 metres, an event in which he was a comparative novice. Drawn in the outside lane in the final, he came hurtling out of his blocks and left the American favourites floundering as he rushed to a new world record of 47.6 seconds. The man who later became a missionary in his birthplace of China had his friendly rivalry with 100 metres gold medallist Harold Abrahams captured in the Oscar-winning film, *Chariots of Fire*.

● It was on the screen as the best known of the Hollywood Tarzans that Johnny Weissmuller was famous in the 1930s. But his early fame came in the Olympic swimming pool. He won 52 US titles, had 28 world records ratified, and was the first man to break the one-minute barrier in the 100 metres and the first to break five minutes in the 440 yards freestyle. Weissmuller, who had taken up swimming to beat a childhood heart ailment, won five gold medals in the pool in the Olympics of 1924 and 1928.

● Spaniard Ricardo Zamora, known throughout the soccer world as 'the Great Zamora', was considered a near unbeatable goalkeeper. An eccentric genius, he boasted that no opponent would get the ball past him in the 1924 Olympic soccer championship. He was right. Spain were knocked out by Italy in a first-round match when the

Spanish captain turned the ball past Zamora into his own net in the last minute. It was the only goal of the game, and 'the Great Zamora' sank to his knees and wept.

● Defending the Olympic middleweight championship he had won in 1920, British boxer Harry Mallin was involved in an extraordinary incident in the 1924 quarter-finals against Frenchman Roger Brousse. In the final round when seemingly ahead on points, Mallin was bitten on the chest by Brousse during a close-quarters clinch. Mallin attempted to protest to the referee, but because of language difficulties could not make himself understood. Brousse was awarded a controversial points decision, but following a complaint from a neutral Swedish official who had seen the biting incident, the boxing committee held an inquiry. They studied the tell-tale teeth marks on Mallin's chest, and disqualified Brousse and reversed the decision. Mallin, a London policeman, went on to retain his title by outpointing his countryman John Elliott in the final. British champion from 1919 to 1923, Mallin went through his career of more than 200 amateur contests without a single defeat ... even by a hungry fighter!

● India, led by army captain Dhyan Chand, won the men's field hockey title in Amsterdam in 1928 without conceding a single goal in the tournament. For the legendary Chand, who used to play in bare feet, it was the first of three Olympic gold medals. Hockey became a major sport in India, and officials approached Mahatma Gandhi to ask for his support on the way to the finals in Los Angeles. His response: 'Hockey? What is hockey?'

● Irish doctor Pat O'Callaghan won the gold medal in the hammer-throwing competition in the 1928 Games in Amsterdam just a year after taking up the event. He retained the title four years later in Los Angeles. Dr O'Callaghan, a magnificent all-rounder, was invited back to Los Angeles fifty-two years later to watch Irish hope Declan Haggerty bid to bring the hammer title back to Ireland. Declan had a nightmare competition, and managed three times to throw the hammer into the side of the cage. As Declan walked miserably away from the throwing circle after his third unsuccessful attempt to register a throw, he went to signal his apologies to Dr O'Callaghan and dropped the hammer on his own foot, breaking a toe.

● According to the records, French discus thrower Jules Noel finished fourth in his event in the 1932 Los Angeles Olympics, although neutral observers were convinced that he had produced a winning throw. Sadly for Jules, the attention of all the field judges had been distracted by an exciting moment in the pole vault, and nobody in authority had seen exactly where the discus landed. Jules was allowed another throw but was unable to challenge the leaders. American John Anderson won with an Olympic record throw of 49.49 metres.

● The 1936 Olympics pole vault competition went on long into the night, and floodlights had to be switched on as American Earle Meadows held off the challenge of Japanese team-mates Shuhei Nishida and Sueo Oe. They finished at exactly the same height after an equal number of attempts, and they refused to vault off against each other for second place. The two vaulting pals drew lots to see who should be placed second in the record books, and Nishida stood in the runner's-up place on the podium and received the silver medal. When they returned to Tokyo they took their medals to a jeweller, who cut them in half length-wise and then fused them back together so that each athlete had a half-bronze, half-silver medal.

● When he was eleven years old, Oliver Halassy was knocked down by a tram in his native Budapest, and had to have his right leg amputated from below the knee. Despite his handicap, he became one of Hungary's greatest swimmers and was a European 1,500 metres champion. But it was in water polo that he made his biggest impact at international level, playing in nearly 100 matches for Hungary. Oliver won an Olympic silver medal in 1928, and gold medals in 1932 and 1936.

● The 1936 football tournament in the Berlin Games heaved with controversy and black comedy. When the German referee ordered off Italian Achille Piccini in a match against the United States he was physically abused by the Italian players. He changed his mind after being pummelled by half a dozen players, and Piccini was still on the field at the end with Italy winners by 1-0 on their way to the gold medal. Peru stormed out of the tournament in protest after they had been ordered to replay their quarter-final against Austria behind closed doors. The Peruvians had won the match 4-2 after extra-time, but during a pitch invasion the Austrians claimed one of their players had been beaten up by Peruvian supporters. Peru took their entire Olympic team home, and the Colombians joined them in a sympathy walk-out.

● An 18-year-old high jumper, Fanny Blankers-Koen finished equal sixth in the 1936 Olympics in Berlin. She was a 30-year-old housewife and a mother of two children by the time the next Games were staged in London in 1948. By then, most athletes would have hung up their spikes, but the 'Flying Dutchwoman' produced a parade of peak performances that earned her four gold medals and a permanent place in Olympic history as one of the greatest women competitors of all time.

Born in Amsterdam in the last year of the First World War, Francina Koen was encouraged to take up athletics by her father after she had revealed all-round sporting talent at school. She used to make a thirty-mile round trip every day by bicycle to train under the guidance of Jan Blankers, an outstanding triple jumper who won the AAA title in London in 1931 and again in 1933. Jan married Fanny in 1940 and continued to coach her. He motivated her for the London Olympics with the deliberate taunt, 'They are saying you are too old, Fanny. Go out and prove them wrong.'

Since the Berlin Games, she had set or equalled world records in the 100 yards, 100 metres, long jump, high jump and 80 metres hurdles. The hardest job was deciding which events to enter in the 1948 Olympics. She settled for the 100 metres, 200 metres and 80 metres hurdles, and she proceeded to win them all over an electrifying span of just nine days during which she competed twelve times in heats and finals and broke the tape in every race. Fanny then completed her gold rush by anchoring the Dutch sprint relay team to victory, taking over the baton in third place and overhauling the leaders with an inspired burst in the last twenty metres.

She was homesick and missed her children so much during the Games that she broke down and wept before being coaxed by her husband to continue her gold rush. After the Games she decided she was going to retire, but the call of the track was too strong. During the next four years she set a new world record for 220 yards, won three titles in the European championships in Brussels, and then switched to the pentathlon and created a new world record.

A blood infection prevented her producing winning form in the 1952 Helsinki Olympics, and she bowed out of competitive athletics as the first lady of the track, continuing to serve her sport in an administrative capacity.

Forty years after her blaze of glory in London, Fanny returned to the scene of her triumph with the author and Brian Moore for the ITV documentary *The Games of '48*. Fanny had us in fits of laughter with her infectious humour, and revealed: 'I nearly blew the fourth gold medal. I went shopping in Oxford Street on the day of the relay final and got held up on the tube. I arrived at Wembley Stadium with just moments to spare, and the team officials were furious with me. But they forgave me when I broke the tape. It was the happiest time of my life.'

● There was a 'Little and Large' show from the American team in the 1948 London Olympics. Bantamweight weightlifting gold medallist Joe di Pietro stood 4ft 6in, and basketball gold medallist Bob Kurland looked down from a height of just over seven feet.

● Hungarian Karoly Takács was a champion right-handed pistol shot in the 1930s, but his career seemed over when he lost his right arm in a grenade explosion. Ten years later in the 1948 Games he won a gold medal – shooting left-handed.

● The judging in the gymnastics competition at the 1948 London Olympics was, to say the least, eccentric. The maximum that can be scored for any one exercise is 10.00. One judge was removed from the panel when she put up a score of 13.1!

● Jean Boiteaux had just won the Olympic 400 metres swimming gold medal for France in the 1952 Games in Helsinki when startled officials were disturbed to see a spectator dive fully clothed into the pool. He swam to where the new champion was recovering his breath and kissed him on both cheeks. No disciplinary action was taken when it was discovered that the invader was Jean's father, who was celebrating his son's victory.

● Yvacheslav Ivanov, a master sculler from Moscow, was so excited about his victory in the single sculls at the 1956 Melbourne Games that he tossed his gold medal high in the air in a gesture of delight. As he reached out to catch his prized possession he succeeded only in knocking it into the waters of Lake Wendouree. The eighteen-year-old Soviet dived into the water, but was unable to retrieve his medal. He was later presented with a replacement medal by the International Olympic Committee. Ivanov received gold medals again in 1960 and 1964 and each time clung on tightly to the greatest award in the world of sport.

● Wim Esajas travelled all the way to the Rome Olympics from Surinam in South America as his country's sole representative in the 1960 Games. His event was on the track in the 800 metres. On the day of his heats Wim rested at the Olympic village in preparation for his afternoon activity on the Olympic track. Unfortunately for Wim, the heats were run in the morning. He was eliminated without setting foot on the track.

● The winner of the light-heavyweight championship in the boxing finals at Rome in 1960 went to bed wearing his gold medal. His name was Cassius Marcellus Clay, who later became even better known in the professional ring as Muhammad Ali. It was in Rome that the world first heard the boast, 'I am the greatest!'

● France scored the only goal of the field hockey match against Belgium in the Rome Olympics while the Belgian players were standing still because the whistle had gone. The umpire awarded a goal, and it transpired that the whistle had been blown by an Italian policeman directing traffic just outside the ground.

● Olympic heroes have rarely come more determined or plucky than Don Thompson, Britain's lone athletics gold medallist in the 1960 Games. He had collapsed with exhaustion in the closing stages of the 50km walk in the 1956 Olympics and had vowed to make proper preparations for the Rome Games four years later. He got himself acclimatised for the sultry summer heat of Italy by turning the bathroom of his home into a steam room where he used to follow a series of explosive exercises while wearing a tracksuit in temperatures of 100 degrees Fahrenheit. The small, bespectacled insurance clerk – dubbed 'Little Mouse' by the press – was rewarded for his thoroughness with an inspiring victory in an Olympic record 4hrs 25mins 30secs.

● American pole vaulter Don Bragg had a burning ambition to follow former Olympic swimming champion Johnny Weissmuller in the film role of Tarzan. After winning the gold medal in the 1960 Games in the Rome Olympics, Bragg delighted the crowd – and amazed his rivals – by celebrating with a Tarzan-style yell. He was signed up to play Tarzan in a Hollywood movie, and was swinging away happily on location when shooting of the film was abandoned because of a legal battle over an alleged copyright infringement. Bragg discovered that Hollywood could be a jungle.

● Defending Olympic javelin champion Elvira Ozolina was so ashamed of her failure to retain her title in the 1964 Tokyo Games that she went straight to the hairdresser in the Olympic village and demanded to have all her hair shaved off. When the hairdresser refused Ozolina took the clippers herself and started cutting her own hair. The hairdresser then took over and shaved off all her hair. Four years earlier the entire Japanese wrestling team had had their heads shaved after a poor performance in the Rome Olympics.

● South Korean flyweight Dong-Kih Choh was so disgusted at his disqualification for punching after having been ordered to 'stop boxing' that he staged a sit-down strike in the ring during the 1964 boxing tournament. Dong-Kih sat cross-legged in the middle of the ring and turned a deaf ear to all pleadings and demands that he should leave. His stubborn squat held up the boxing programme for nearly an hour. He was finally persuaded to leave after a promise had been made to him that an inquiry would be held into his disqualification. Mr Choh took no further part in the tournament. His sit-in protest was beaten by 16 minutes by his bantamweight countryman Byun Jong-Il in Seoul in 1988. He squatted for 67 minutes after a disputed points defeat that led to New Zealand referee Keith Walker being attacked and punched by incensed members of the Korean team. Walker was smuggled out of the stadium and went straight home.

● Al Oerter well merited his nickname 'The Man with the Golden Arm' by winning four successive gold medals in the discus, one for each of his four children. His extraordinary competitive powers were best illustrated in the 1964 Tokyo Olympics when he completed his hat-trick despite being doubly handicapped by the pain of a pinched nerve in his back and a torn rib cartilage. Standing 6ft 4in and weighing eighteen stone, Oerter won his first gold medal at the 1956 Olympics in Melbourne when a twenty-year-old outsider and just two years after breaking the American high school record. He made it a unique four triumphs in a row in Mexico in 1968 with a lifetime's best throw of 212ft 5in. The New York-born computer programme analyst broke the world record four times and made a comeback at forty with a fifth gold medal in mind, a dream that died with the American boycott of the Moscow Olympics.

● British boxer Chris Finnegan won the gold medal in the middleweight division in the 1968 Games in Mexico, but it was eight hours after the final that he was officially confirmed as champion. He was unable to supply a sample for the urine test, and two Olympic officials had to accompany him until the early hours of the morning. It took eight pints of beer before Chris could oblige.

● Ralph Boston, 1960 Olympic long jump champion, did not realise just how prophetic he was being when he said before the 1968 competition, 'Don't get Bob Beamon mad or he's liable to jump clean out of the pit.' Beamon did exactly that with his first jump, becoming not only the first man to break the 28-foot barrier but also the 29-foot mark. It was the shortest *competition* in Olympic history. Nobody could get anywhere near the new world record, and Beamon took only one more jump before retiring to the shelter of the grandstand to escape the rain that came cascading down immediately after his winning leap.

● BBC commentator David Coleman got so carried away with David Hemery's magnificent world record breaking run to the gold medal in the 1968 400 metres hurdles final that he shouted, 'Who cares who's third.' Meantime, Britain's John Sherwood was hurling himself over the finishing line for a marvellous bronze medal. The Coleman clanger was edited out of later recordings of the race.

● The 1968 football final between Hungary and Bulgaria developed into farce when the referee ordered off three Bulgarians during the closing minutes of the first half. It became a more even game in the second half when a Hungarian was sent off. The ten men of Hungary eventually beat the eight men of Bulgaria 4-1.

● The Japanese laid down their sticks and walked off in protest after a penalty stroke had been awarded to India in a preliminary match in the 1968 men's field hockey tournament.

● The Pakistani team and officials were so incensed by their disputed 1-0 defeat by host country West Germany in the men's field hockey final in the 1972 Games that they stormed the judges' table. Water was poured over the official in charge, and several of the Pakistani players refused to face the German flag during the playing of the German national anthem at the medal ceremony. The entire Pakistani team was banned for life by the International Olympic Committee, a sentence that was later lifted.

● Television commentators were baffled by the identity of the leading rider in the 125-mile road cycling race in the 1972 Games. It transpired that his name was Batty Flynn, and he was an Irishman who, with three team-mates, had joined the race after the start. They were making a protest at Ireland's exclusion from the cycling.

● A world record came with every one of the seven gold medals won by Mark Spitz in the swimming pool in the 1972 Games in Munich. When collecting his third gold medal, Spitz waved his poolside shoes in the direction of the press photographers. The Russians demanded that he should be disqualified for breaking his amateur status by advertising the manufacturers' trademark, but the International Olympic Committee threw out the complaint.

● Haseley Crawford, winner of the 100 metres gold medal in the 1976 Olympics in Montreal, pulled up with an attack of cramp in the 200 metres final. He fell to the track clutching his leg, and then slowly jogged to the finishing line. It was noted on the video replays that he never actually left his lane, and his time from gun to tape was officially recorded as 1min 19.6secs.

● Two British yachtsmen, Alan Warren and David Hunt – noted for their zany and sometimes eccentric humour – went overboard with their jokes during the 1976 Games. They posed as naval officers working on behalf of the Queen and 'screened' the Canadian police who had been appointed as Her Majesty's bodyguards. They saved their biggest laugh for the actual competition. The pair were so disillusioned after their Tempest class yacht, Gift 'Orse, had broken down for the third time that they set light to it, and sat in a dinghy watching it burn until a coastguard cutter rammed it and sent it to the bottom of Lake Ontario. Hunt, crewman to Warren, told astonished press reporters, 'My skipper is lacking in style. I told him his place as the captain was with the ship, but, shamefully, he refused to go down with it.'

● Olmeus Charles, of Haiti, held the Olympic stage longer than any other track runner in the 1976 Games. He ambled around the track in the 10,000 metres and finished in just over forty-two minutes, the slowest time ever recorded in the Olympics. It later transpired that he had never before set foot on a track in an international meeting, and he had been given the trip to Montreal as reward for enterprising office work. His team-mate Wilnor Joseph finished the second heat of the 800 metres in 2mins 15.26secs, a time so slow that it would not have qualified him for the 800 metres final in the 1900 Games! But at least Baron de Coubertin, founder of the modern Olympics, would have approved. This truly was the spirit of taking part rather than winning!

● Boris Onischenko, an army major from the Ukraine, was one of the world's most prominent modern pentathletes who was particularly successful in the fencing discipline. His British opponent in the 1976 Games, Adrian Parker, was convinced he had not been hit by Onischenko, yet his automatic light register lit up. Parker's team-mate, Jeremy Fox, had the same experience and the jury were asked to examine Onischenko's épeé. It was discovered that it had been wired with a hidden push-button circuit breaker which enabled Onischenko to register hits at will. He was disqualified and sent back to the Soviet Union in disgrace.

● Japanese gymnast Shun Fujimoto proved himself one of the bravest of all Olympic competitors at Montreal in 1976. He broke his leg at the knee in his final somersault in the floor exercise, but insisted on continuing to compete. He performed his side horse exercises, and then went through his routine on the rings. It was when he dismounted from the rings for an excruciatingly painful landing that he finally had to concede that his Olympics were over.

● Has there ever been a more jinxed or more accident-prone athlete than Cuban sprinter Silvio Leonard? He pulled a muscle as he crossed the finishing line in the 1975 Pan-American 100 metres final and, as he hobbled forward in pain, was unable to stop himself falling into the ten-foot moat surrounding the track. Leonard recovered from his injuries in time to travel with the Cuban team to the Montreal Olympics where, a week before his heats, he trod on a broken perfume bottle and cut his foot so badly he was unable to produce his best form. Four years later in the 100 metres final in the Moscow Games, he was beaten by the bat of an eyelid in a photo-finish with Britain's Allan Wells for the gold medal.

● A lot of the world's top javelin throwers got the wind up over what they claimed were unfair tactics by the Russians during the 1980 Olympics in Moscow. It was alleged that every time a Soviet thrower was preparing to run up during the men's javelin event the huge stadium doors behind them would be opened to give them the full benefit of a following wind. The doors, it was claimed, were then closed when a non-Soviet javelin competitor took his throw. The Soviet Union got a surprise first and second place, and a lot of throwers reckoned their chances had gone with the wind.

● Seven walkers were disqualified for 'lifting' during the 20km walk in the 1980 Moscow Olympics. There was no danger of Thipsamay Chanthapone, of Laos, being accused of going too quickly. Looking for all the world as if he was on an afternoon stroll, he kept both feet firmly on the ground and finished more than half an hour behind the field in a glorious last place that brought him a standing ovation when his walk finally finished.

● Rain seemed a certainty as the spectators fled into the impressive Lenin Stadium for the opening ceremony. Then, just twelve minutes after the first parade, the dark clouds cleared and hazy sun broke through. The Soviet organisers later revealed that six specially fitted aeroplanes had sprayed the sky with chemicals to clear the threatening clouds.

● Alwyn Morris, a Mohawk Indian from the Caughawaga Reserve in Quebec, partnered Hugh Fisher in the Kayak Pairs in the 1984 Games in Los Angeles. Morris carried with him a beautifully decorated eagle feather, and after the Canadian pair had won the gold medal he explained, 'This feather symbolises the sharing of our victory with the native people of North America.'

● Four-year-old Alex Baumann's Czechoslovakian parents took him to Canada in 1968 when Russian tanks rolled into Prague. Sixteen years later in Los Angeles he won Canada's first swimming gold medal since 1912 when he took the 400 metres individual medley in a world record time. Baumann was sinking beers for two hours in a bid to produce his urine sample when the medical officials realised he was under age and ordered him to switch to non-alcoholic assistance!

● Matt Biondi climbed out of the pool after winning the 100 metres freestyle for the United States in 1988 and told the NBC-TV interviewer: 'When I get home the first thing I'll do is go to Disneyland.' Before the interview ended, he said: 'Later, I'm going to Disney World.' An IOC official overheard the interview and ordered NBC to destroy the tape because of what was seen as blatant advertising. It was sarcastically suggested: 'These have become the Mickey Mouse Games.' Biondi continued his golden splash into 1992 and took his Olympic medals haul to eleven in the Barcelona pool, tying the all-time record held by Mark Spitz.

● All members of the Korean judo team at the 1988 Seoul Game made midnight visits to a cemetery where they sat for an hour gathering strength from the spirits. They collected two gold medals.

● The tiny Pacific island nation of Vanuatu proudly sent their first ever competitor to the Olympics. Their chosen representative was a boxer called Eduard Paululum, and he went to Seoul in 1988 to challenge for the bantamweight championship. On the morning of his first contest Eduard ate a hearty breakfast ... too hearty by all accounts because he failed to make the weight when he went to the scales and was eliminated without throwing a punch.

● Florence Griffith Joyner, sprint queen of the 1988 Olympics in Seoul, was asked after her world record breaking runs in the 100 and 200 metres whether she took the eye with her speed when she was young. 'I was pretty quick,' she said, 'but I was best known locally for the fact that I used to go to the shops wearing my pet boa constrictor like a muffler.'

● In 1990, American sprint hurdler Gail Devers was told by doctors that she might have to have both her feet amputated. They had become badly infected after an overdose of radiation therapy to treat a thyroid condition. But following a new emergency course of medication she came off the danger list. Two years later Gail struck a gold on the track at the 1992 Barcelona Olympics, winning the 100 metres. Only a crashing fall prevented her completing a golden double in the 100 metres hurdles. Gail collected a second gold medal as a member of the USA sprint relay team.

● Britain's Derek Redmond produced an amazing display of courage in the men's 400 metres on the Barcelona track. He pulled a hamstring soon after the start and, despite appalling pain, limped round to finish the race. A spectator ran towards him, and as security guards tried to prevent him reaching the stricken runner Redmond waved them away. The man was his father, and Derek leant on his shoulder as he hobbled round the track for the slowest but most emotional 400 metres in Olympic history. 'I was determined to finish what I had started,' said a tearful Redmond as the crowd rose to applaud his bravery.

● Eleven weeks before the Barcelona Games Canadian sculler Silken Laumann had been written out of the Olympics because of the little matter that her right leg was thigh high in plaster after she had sustained a double fracture and a severed muscle. Silken was told that her competitive rowing days were over. She demanded that the doctors order her plaster to be removed, and within a month of her accident – a collision during a race in Germany – she was back in a boat training for the Olympics. She provided a golden finish to the story by finishing first in the single sculls in Barcelona, using a walking stick to help her climb on to the winners' podium.

It is not only the Olympics that can be game for a laugh. There have been some strange happenings on and off the pitch in World Cup tournaments, as this collection of footballing oddities reveals:

● The United States trainer raced on to the pitch to treat an injured player during the 1930 semi-final against Argentina. He stumbled and dropped his box of medical supplies and a bottle of chloroform smashed on the pitch. The trainer took the fumes full in the face as he bent to pick up the box. He folded slowly to the ground like a puppet that has had its strings cut, and had to be carried back to the touchline bench.

● Uruguay and Argentina both insisted on using a 'home' manufactured ball in the first World Cup Final in Montevideo in 1930. Belgian referee John Langenus, resplendent in knickerbockers and a natty striped tie, came out for the kick-off with a ball under each arm, one made in Argentina and the other in Uruguay. The two captains tossed, Manuel Ferreira winning the right for Argentina to use *their* ball for the first 45 minutes. Uruguay, 2-1 down at half-time, used *their* ball in the second-half and won the match 4-2.

● 'By Royal Appointment' took on a new meaning when Romania entered the first World Cup tournament in Uruguay in 1930. King Carol II insisted that a representative team be sent after the invitation to play had at first been turned down because the players could not get the necessary three months off work. The King selected the team himself and then arranged time off for each of the players with full pay. They were eliminated from the tournament after playing just two matches. Only 300 spectators watched their match against Peru. When King Carol was overthrown in 1940 he fled to South America where he was warmly remembered as the 'football mad' king.

● Hector Castro, scorer of Uruguay's victory-clinching fourth goal in the 1930 Final, had only one hand. He had lost his hand and part of his arm in a childhood accident.

● Ten charted boats spilling over with Argentinian supporters sailed across the River Plate to Montevideo for the 1930 World Cup Final. Only the first two to sail docked in time for the passengers to see the game. The other eight were delayed by thick fog. Match referee John Langenus was aboard the first of the boats.

● Captain Alex Villaplane proudly led out France against Mexico for the first ever World Cup match on Sunday afternoon, 13 July, 1930, the day before Bastille Day. Fifteen years later the same Alex Villaplane was shot by French resistance fighters for allegedly collaborating with the Nazis during the Second World War.

● Argentinian-born Raimondo Orsi scored a spectacular goal for Italy against Czechoslovakia in the 1934 Final, his right-foot shot sending the ball on a curling trail into the net. The day after the Final Orsi tried more than 20 times to repeat the shot for the benefit of photographers. He failed every time.

● Swiss centre-forward Poldi Kielholz, scorer of three goals in the 1934 finals tournament, wore spectacles.

● Mexico made the long trek to Italy for the 1934 tournament, lost to the United States in a qualifying match, and returned home without playing a single game in the finals.

● Leonidas da Silva, flamboyant star of Brazil's 1938 attack, was unhappy playing against Poland on the muddy pitch at Strasbourg. He decided he would have better footing if he went back to his boyhood days and played barefooted. But the moment he removed his boots and tossed them nonchalantly over the touchline, the referee ordered him to put them back on because it was in contravention of the rules of the game to play without boots. The dramatic match was held up while Leonidas replaced his boots and he was sure-footed enough to score four goals in a remarkable 6-5 victory. Ernest Willimowski scored four goals for Poland and finished on the losing side.

● Italian skipper Giuseppe 'Peppino' Meazza had that sinking feeling as he scored the semi-final penalty against Brazil that clinched a place in the 1938 Final. As he steered the spot-kick into the net his shorts, torn earlier in the game, slipped down to leave him exposed. His celebrating team-mates hid his blushes until a new pair was produced. Milan's magnificent San Siro ground was renamed the Gieuseppe Meazza Stadium in honour of the Italian World Cup hero.

● With war clouds gathering over Europe, Jules Rimet – then President of FIFA and the man after whom the World Cup trophy was named – reclaimed the trophy from the

Italian FA. He thought long and hard about where it would be safest and decided, with what was perhaps typical French logic, that the only place was the bedroom. For the duration of the Second World War the Jules Rimet trophy nestled under his bed.

● Austria beat Switzerland 7-5 in an astonishing quarter-finals match at Lausanne in the 1954 tournament. The Swiss came up with an unusual reason for some eccentric play by goalkeeper Eugene Parlier. It was a blistering-hot day and it was announced after the match that Parlier had been suffering from sunstroke.

● Juan Hohberg scored an 87th minute equaliser for Uruguay against Hungary in the 1954 semi-finals. His team-mates overdid their celebrating and goal hero Hohberg was knocked out under the weight of their congratulations. He recovered in time to join in the extra-time session during which he shot against a post before Hungary forced a 4-2 victory.

● Scotland suddenly became the team without a manager when Andy Beattie announced his resignation after the Scots had gone down 1-0 to Austria in their opening match in the 1954 finals. Beattie felt that he was not being allowed to manage by the Scottish selectors. The Scots were beaten 7-0 by Uruguay on a scorching hot day in their final match in the tournament. Right-half Tommy Docherty said: 'We got such a run-around that we were suffering from sunburned tongues!' It was the first World Cup match screened live on Scottish television.

● Northern Ireland, surprise qualifiers at the expense of Italy, brought humour as well as skill and endeavour to the 1958 finals. In trainer Gerry Morgan, a lovable little character with a Jimmy Durante profile and rakishly worn headgear, they had one of the great personalities of the tournament. He regaled visitors from the world's press corps with a procession of blarney-based stories that sent them away happy if incredulous. One newspaperman wrote that the Irish players had trained on a diet of whisky and potato sandwiches. Another reported that the Irish players were on a £1,000-a-man win bonus, when the actual figure was £10. Morgan convinced reporters that skipper Danny Blanchflower had been promised a knighthood by the Queen if he collected the Cup. It was Blanchflower who told startled reporters that Ireland's secret tactic was always 'to equalise before the opposition scores.' The Irish had a party after every match, win, lose or draw. A foreign journalist walked into a swinging party after a 3-1 defeat by Argentina. 'What are you celebrating?' he asked manager Peter Doherty. 'Oh, we're just drowning our sorrows,' he replied with a wide grin. The Irish laughed their way through to the quarter-finals.

● Jimmy Greaves had a dog named after him during the 1962 finals in Chile. A stray mongrel ran on to the pitch during the Brazil-England match. Jimmy went down on his knees to collect it after it had run loose around the pitch for three minutes. As he carried it to the touchline the dog relieved itself all the way down Jimmy's England shirt. Animal-loving Garrincha claimed the dog after the match. He called it 'Jimmy' and took it home with him to Brazil.

● Swiss forward Norbert Eschmann was brought down by West Germany's Horst Szymaniak in a 1962 World Cup match. He was treated on the touchline for seventeen minutes in what were pre-substitute days, and he then returned to the action. An x-ray after the match showed that he had an ankle fracture.

● Pele was so pleased with the two-goal debut of his deputy Amarildo for Brazil against Spain in the 1962 World Cup finals that he jumped fully clothed into the team bath after the match to congratulate him. During his astonishing career, the peerless Pele scored more than 1,000 goals. He played for Brazil in the winning 1958 and 1970 teams, and missed the 1962 Final after damaging a muscle in the opening match. In the 1966 finals, he was ruthlessly kicked out of the tournament by defenders who took their orders to mark him too literally. In his peak years, Pele was rated so highly that the Brazilian government declared that he was a national treasure.

● There have been five sets of brothers who have featured together in World Cup Final teams. The first brothers to win World Cup medals were Germany's Fritz and Ottmar Walter in 1954. The Evaristo brothers, Juan and Mario, were runners-up with Argentina in 1930 and the van der Kerkhof twins – Willy and René – played together for Holland against Argentina in 1978. Bobby and Jack Charlton were, relatively speaking, the best known brothers who helped England win the World Cup in 1966. The last brothers to appear together in a World Cup Final were Bernd and Karl-Heinz Forster, who were runners-up with West Germany in 1982. Cameroon's Biyick brothers had mixed fortunes in the opening match of the 1990 finals against Argentina. Kana was ordered off in the 60th minute and four minutes later his brother, Omam, headed the winning goal against the defending champions.

● In 1966 the World Cup had its first four-legged hero. The Jules Rimet trophy was stolen while on exhibition at a stamp show in Central Hall, Westminster. There was a massive police and public hunt for the missing trophy and, just when it looked as if football's number one prize had disappeared into the smelter's pot, it was unearthed by a dog called Pickles, who sniffed it out from its hiding place under a bush in Norwood, South London. Pickles and his owner collected a £6,000 reward and a man who had demanded a £15,000 ransom for the return of the trophy was jailed for two years. Brazil won the Jules Rimet trophy outright with their third victory in Mexico in 1970. Thirteen years later they had to replace it with a replica after thieves stole it and melted it down.

● Alan Ball was so bitterly disappointed by England's extra-time defeat by West Germany in the 1970 quarter-finals that he threw his tournament medal out of his hotel bedroom window. England, leading 2-0, eventually lost 3-2 after extra time. Goalkeeper Gordon Banks missed the match because of a stomach complaint, and later voiced suspicions that he had been deliberately 'nobbled' by somebody slipping him a dodgy drink.

● The West Germans staged a spectacular opening ceremony in the 1974 finals that involved meticulous organisation. But they had overlooked one minor detail. As Brazil and Yugoslavia lined up for the kick-off to the opening match in the stadium at Frankfurt, the referee delayed the start while embarrassed officials hustled around the pitch putting in the corner and centre-line flags.

● At the start of the 1974 finals, a German company provided each squad with a luxury coach to shuttle them to and from matches and training grounds. After Zaire had been eliminated, a representative of the coach company called to collect the bus – only to be told that the squad had already left in the coach, bound for Africa.

● Hungary's Laszlo Kiss scored the fastest hat-trick in World Cup history against El Salvador in 1982. He found the net three times in nine minutes ... after coming on as a substitute.

● Italian striker Paolo Rossi won the 'Golden Boot' as top scorer in the 1982 finals. It was hailed as a vintage performance back home where Pescara-based wine-growers presented him with 1,000 bottles of wine.

● The 1990 finals in Italy had a world-wide television audience of 31 billion viewers. More than half the world's population watched at least one match. Football fans in Thailand were not impressed with their coverage. Viewers had to sit through 40 commercial breaks during each match. The biggest riot of the 1990 World Cup took place not in Sicily, but in India. Hundreds of football followers in Calcutta marched on the government electrical power headquarters and attacked department officials after power cuts had blacked out television World Cup action.

● The Cameroon players were weighed down during the 1990 finals with good luck charms given to them by witch doctors, who were forbidden from treating any injured players in case they broke FIFA's strict laws on the use of drugs. There has been concern about the influence of witch doctors on African football since a team from Zimbabwe was banned after taking part in a ritual just before a match. They urinated in unison on the pitch in full view of the spectators and disbelieving photographers.

● While things ran like a well-oiled engine on the pitch for West German manager Franz Beckenbauer, he had his troubles off the field. While he was plotting tactics for the second round match against Holland, a car thief drove off in his £70,000 Mercedes.

● The Dutch post office were licked along with Holland's players when they were eliminated by West Germany. They had ambitiously printed in advance of the match the first one million stamps of a special 16-million issue to mark a Dutch victory in the tournament. The million stamps, carrying the inscription 'Netherlands World Champions 1990', were scrapped. It was suggested they should play the Last Post.

● We saw the first case of a substitute goal in the 1994 finals in the United States. A Mexican defender fell into the back of the net against Bulgaria, and the stanchion collapsed. The game was held up for five minutes while a replacement goal was brought on. Six workmen wheeled the new goal the length of the pitch, and then they hammered it into the ground while the 'injured' goal was wheeled away for treatment.

● German manager Berti Vogts came up with a novel way to beat the oven heat in the first round of the 1994 finals in the USA. He told his players without a flicker of a smile, 'You should all run around more to create a draught.'

● Boris Mihailov, Bulgaria's goalkeeper hero in their spirited run through to the 1994 semi-finals, provided some bald facts for the World Cup reporters. When asked how it was that in the qualifying rounds he had been severely follically challenged yet had a fine head of hair by the time of the finals, he revealed that he had undergone a hair transplant. It had cost him £20,000, half his year's salary with French Second Division side Mulhouse.

● World Cup fever caught on right across the globe during World Cup '94. Iran's government allowed the tournament to be screened on television for the first time in 16 years. However, since the competition was in the West, and since there was the chance that women spectators in the crowd might wear something revealing under the blistering sun, Iranian censors inserted Islamically correct crowd scenes that had spectators dressed like Sherpas, eyeball-deep with furs! In Thailand, bank robbers carried a huge safe stuffed with cash past a night guard as he watched the World Cup on television. At the Hyundai factory 21,000 workers called a two-hour strike, downing tools long enough to watch South Korea against Spain.

● Each Saudi player received a Mercedes and a Volvo plus a $50,000 bonus for beating Morocco and Belgium in the first round of the 1994 finals. There was a Rolls Royce and $100,000 waiting for them if they had beaten Sweden in the second stage, but they went down to a 3-1 defeat.

● When spectators booed German midfield player Stefan Effenberg, he responded with a Harvey von Smith two-fingered salute during the 1994 finals. Manager Bertie Vogts reacted not with two fingers but with the boot, and Effenberg was kicked out of the squad.

● An Albanian was reported during World Cup '94 to have wagered his wife on Argentina beating Romania. The Romanians won, and the gambler lost his wife!

● There was double agony for German left-back Martin Wagner in the 1994 finals. He was knocked out with his side leading 1-0 against Bulgaria in the quarter finals. When he came round the score was 2-1. 'Who scored our second goal?' asked Wagner, not knowing that the Bulgarians had won to reach the semi-finals.

● Did the World Cup in the United States convince the Americans that 'the beautiful game' was worth adopting as a major sport? This is how a newspaper correspondent in Chicago put it: 'As an advertisement to convert our Soccer-challenged nation to the global game, this was like trying to sell dentistry by advertising the anaesthetic.'

4: Hark Who's Talking

I first started collecting off-beat sporting quotes for a *Daily Herald* column in 1962. These are among my favourites, with the cricketers going in first to bat.

“When I win the toss on a good pitch, I bat. When I win the toss on a doubtful pitch I think about it a bit and then I bat. When I win the toss on a very bad pitch, I think about it a bit longer and then I bat.”

– **W.G. Grace**

“I'm not ecstatic about paying £1,000 for 20 minutes in the air. It is more than commercial rates and in these days of deregulation it is a scandal.”

– **David Gower,**
on his fine for his 'Biggles' escapade

“I used to bowl tripe, then I wrote it, now I sell it.”

– **Arthur Mailey,**
Australian leg-spinner, journalist and butcher

“Good morning Peter, good morning Roy.”

– **Alec Bedser,**
England's chairman of selectors, greeting John Lever and Ray East on the morning of a Test trial

❝It's rather like sending your opening batsman to the crease only to find the moment the first balls are bowled that their bats have been broken before the game by the team captain.❞

– **Sir Geoffrey Howe,**
in his resignation speech to the House

❝Blimey, the bugger can't bend as well, can he?❞

– **Brian Close,**
on 6ft 8in West Indian fast bowler Joel Garner

❝And let's not forget Malcolm Devon.❞

– **Ted Dexter,**
the then chairman of England's selectors

❝It's like climbing Mount Everest and pulling a hamstring in the last stride.❞

– **Martin Crowe,**
on being dismissed for 299

❝You can count the number of books I have read on one hand. In fact, I don't even think you would fill one hand.❞

– **Jeff Thomson**

❝The only difference between Gooch's tour and what happened on the *Bounty* was that Captain Bligh got that bit more support.❞

– **Greg Chappell,**
on England's disastrous tour of Australia in 1990-91

❝One viewer told me the other day that listening to my old mate Jim Laker and his new sidekick Bob Willis was better than taking two Mogadon.❞

– **Fred Trueman**

"Micky Stewart said the England players do not think about defeat. Some of them do not seem to think very much at all."

– **Mike Selvey**

"Cricket needs brightening up a bit. My solution is to let players drink at the beginning of the game, not after. It always works in our picnic matches."

– **Paul Hogan**

"Ted Dexter and I both speak English, although obviously not the same version."

– **David Gower,**
after Dexter denied sacking him

"I'd rather face Dennis Lillee with a stick of rhubarb than go through all that again."

– **Ian Botham,**
after an appearance in court on assault charges

"If there is a revolution in this country I'd now be in the first 10,000 to the guillotine but not the first 1,000."

– **John Warr,**
on being elected MCC President

"Unless I'm crackers or something, I've scored a bloody sight more runs than that bearded old bugger."

– **Geoff Boycott,**
questioning the legendary status of W.G. Grace

"It's difficult to be more laid back without being actually comatose."

– **Frances Edmonds,**
Phil's wife on David Gower

“At one stage I was out on the balcony with captain Mike Gatting trying to count the number of Pakistani players on the field. But I gave up counting because I don’t carry a calculator.”

– **Micky Stewart,**
England’s manager after accusing Pakistan of time-wasting by the use of substitutes

“This could be your last Test!”

– **The Oval crowd,**
after Phil Edmonds asked them to give him some encouraging support

“A cricket tour in Australia would be the most delightful period in one’s life, if one was deaf.”

– **Harold Larwood**

“Ian Botham couldn’t bowl a hoop downhill.”

– **Fred Trueman**

“It’s all a matter of inches – those between your ears.”

– **Arthur Milton,**
Gloucestershire batsman on spin bowling

“The hallmark of a great captain is the ability to win the toss at the right time.”

– **Richie Benaud**

“If you want a straight answer, it’s maybe yes, maybe no.”

– **Alan Smith,**
Test and County Cricket Board Chief executive

"They're a bunch of gin-soaked old dodderers."

– **Ian Botham,**
on the England selectors

"I believe, in cricketing terms, Graeme Pollock was a sadist."

– **Eddie Barlow**

"I don't like defensive strokes. You can only get three out of them!"

– **W.G. Grace**

"Yes ... no ... maybe ... wait ... yes ... no ..."

– **Denis Compton,**
negotiating a quick single

"You should treat women the same way as any good Yorkshire batsman used to treat a cricket ball. Don't stroke 'em, don't tickle 'em, just give 'em a ruddy good belt!"

– **Fred Trueman**

"If what the England selection committee came up with for the Trent Bridge Test is rebuilding, I don't want them doing my renovations."

– **Ian Chappell,**
after a re-vamped England team lost to Australia by an innings and 180 runs

"He who strokes the ball with loving care is a gentleman. He who studies it with hawk eyes is a worried man. He who blocks fast bowlers and blocks spinners is a wise man."

– **Peter Roebuck**

❝I had a letter from this bloke in Scotland the other day. 'Don't worry,' he wrote. 'It's not your fault. It's the ball's.' He went on for ten pages explaining that no two golf balls had the same centre of gravity and that's why my putts veer away. So it's not me, gentlemen. It's the ball.❞

– **Tony Jacklin,**
giving a light-hearted explanation at a press conference for his lean spell following his back-to-back triumphs in the British and US Open championships

❝There, looking solemnly down on the proceedings at the 16th green, are two spectators who don't give a hoot for The Masters.❞

– **Henry Longhurst,**
the master of the microphone when a shot of two owls sitting in a tree came up on the screen during the 1976 US Masters tournament

❝If you're going to throw a club in temper, it's important to throw it ahead of you in the direction of the green. That way you don't waste energy going back to pick it up.❞

– **Tommy Bolt,**
who was so notorious for his club-throwing tantrums that he was nicknamed 'Thunderbolt'

❝I owe a lot to my parents – especially my mother and father.❞

– **Greg Norman**

“Oh well, no matter what happens I can always dig ditches for a living.”

– Arnold Palmer,
talking during a rare losing run

“I'm going to win so much this year that even my caddie will make it into the top twenty money-winners list.”

– Lee Trevino

“If I put the ball where I can see it, I can't reach it. If I put it where I can reach it, I can't see it.”

– Jackie Gleason,
the rotund comedian on his golfing problems

“Maybe I should go to a sports shop and buy a trophy. That's the only way I'm going to get one.”

– Seve Ballesteros,
talking at St Andrews on the eve of the 1984 Open which, of course, he won

“If I wasn't a professional golfer you wouldn't catch me playing the game if they paid me.”

– Christy O'Connor

“It's a big advantage to be left-handed. Nobody knows enough about your swing to be able to mess you up with advice.”

– Bob Charles

“I learn English from American pros. That's why I speak so bad. I call it PGA English.”

– Roberto De Vicenzo,
apologising for his fractured English

“You always have butterflies in your stomach but these butterflies are playing hockey.”

– **Mike Reid,**
leader of the 1989 US PGA Championship, going into the final round

“I think those golfers who look as though they got dressed in the dark should be penalised two strokes each for offending the public eye.”

– **Doug Sanders**

“We have no restrictions at the Royal and Ancient except that it's a male club.”

– **Michael Bonallack,**
Royal and Ancient secretary

“Ian Woosnam will be a great golfer when he grows up!”

– **Seve Ballesteros,**
after 'little Woosie' had won the Suntory World Match Play Championship

“Ninety-five per cent of putts which finish short don't go in.”

– **Hubert Green**

“Muirfield without a wind is like a lady undressed. There's no challenge.”

– **Tom Watson**

“Why would I want to be out there with all those young guns? No sense playing the flat bellies when you can play the round bellies.”

– **Lee Trevino,**
celebrating his 50th birthday and switching to the lucrative US Seniors tour

“If you watch a game, it's fun. If you play it, it's recreation. If you work at it, it's golf.”

– **Bob Hope**

“Sometimes I think he needs a good kick up the backside. People are too nice to him.”

– **Jolande Lyle,**
on her husband Sandy

“At my first Masters, I got the feeling that if I didn't play well, I wouldn't go to heaven.”

– **Dave Marr**

“Only God could have got out of that one, and even He would have had to throw the ball.”

– **Arnold Palmer,**
after taking five shots to get out of a bunker in The Open

“He's longer than Fred Couples, he's longer than Greg Norman, he's even longer than *War And Peace*!”

– **Bob Verdi,**
of the Chicago Tribune, on John Daly

“Golf is an ineffectual attempt to direct an uncontrollable sphere into an inaccessible hole with instruments ill-adapted to the purpose.”

– **Sir Winston Churchill**

“This game is eighty per cent mental and if you can conquer it mentally you've got half of it beat.”

– **Betty Richardson,**
amateur golfer

❝The way I putted, I must've been reading the greens in Spanish and putting them in English.❞

– **Homero Blancas**

❝I once shot a wild, charging elephant in Africa and it kept coming at me until dropping to the ground at my feet. I wasn't a bit scared. It takes a four-foot putt to scare me to death.❞

– **Sam Snead**

❝The only place Seve turns up for nothing is at his mother's for breakfast.❞

– **Howard Clark**
on Seve Ballesteros

❝Never hurry, never worry and be sure to smell the flowers along the way.❞

– **Walter Hagen**

❝The players' car park is too far away. The practice ground is no good. The place is full of kids. The weather is grotty and last year the courtesy car refused to bring my wife into town.❞

– **Mark James,**
doing a Victor Meldrew impression as he explained why he declined to compete in the 1989 Irish Open

❝I just stand there and hit it!❞

– **Ian Woosnam,**
on his technique

❝I'm not saying my golf game went bad, but if I grew tomatoes they'd come up sliced.❞

– **Lee Trevino**

“I can see the carrot at the end of the tunnel.”
– **Stuart Pearce**

“If you can't join them, beat them!” –
Mr Ellemann-Jensen,
the Danish Foreign Minister, after his country opted out of the Maastricht Treaty and won the European Championships in the same week

“I look at some of the people around today and I bloody well weep. That Mark Hateley; they're talking about spending millions on him and the poor bloke can't play the game. Couldn't trap a dead rat, yet he's made a fortune.”
– **Stan 'the man' Bowles,**
speaks his mind

“Look laddie, if you're in the penalty area and aren't quite sure what to do with the ball, just stick it in the net and we'll discuss all your options afterwards.”
– **Bill Shankly,**
to a goal-shy striker

“I get seventy letters a week asking for advice. I'm the Marjorie Proops of diabetes!”
– **Gary Mabbutt**

“I'm one of those twenty-year, hard graft, overnight successes.”
– **Howard Wilkinson**

“Do I not like that!”

– **Graham Taylor,**
enters the quotation hall of fame during England's unsuccessful World Cup qualifying campaign

“Managing a national team can only be a part-time job. When the Irish FA got me, they always knew they were getting a fisherman.”

– **Jack Charlton**

“He is accused of being arrogant, unable to cope with the press, and a boozer. Sounds like he's got a chance to me.”

– **George Best,**
on Paul Gascoigne

“If you ask me, Kenny Dalglish has about as much personality as a tennis racquet.”

– **Mick Channon**

“I'm not as nice as all that. In fact I swore only last week.”

– **Gary Lineker**

“When Cookie sold you a dummy, you had to pay to get back into the ground.”

– **Jim Baxter,**
on Scottish ball player Charlie Cooke

“No one can turn round and say of me 'His pace has gone.' I never had any. I've got plodding legs.”

– **Ray Wilkins**

“He's very deceptive. He's even slower than he looks.”

– **Tommy Docherty,**
on Welsh international winger Leighton James

"We ended up playing football, and that doesn't suit our style."

– **Alex MacDonald,**
the Airdrie manager gives a unique excuse after his team are beaten

"We shall set out to be as positive as we can, and look to pick up a point."

– **Bobby Robson**

"A lot of people in football don't have much time for the press; they say they're amateurs. But I say to those people, 'Noah was an amateur, but the *Titanic* was built by professionals!'"

– **Malcolm Allison**

"I'd kick my own brother if necessary. That's what being a professional is all about."

– **Steve McMahon**

"Robson for England? He gets injured just at the mere thought of it."

– **Alex Ferguson,**
on Bryan Robson's international prospects in 1992

"Coping with the Italian language shouldn't be a problem. I can't speak English properly yet."

– **Paul Gascoigne**

"I'd like to grab him by the balls and strangle him. Have you ever seen anything like him in your bloody life?"

– **Brian Clough,**
sitting on the fence as usual with his opinion of Sports Minister Colin Moynihan

“That Wheelbarrow, he’s not very fast but he’s nippy.”
– **Bob Paisley,**
on Newcastle United’s Stuart Barrowclough

“It’s like seeing Scotland score a goal. You never quite get used to it.”
– **Rod Stewart,**
on the birth of his daughter

“If they pay peanuts, they can expect monkeys.”
– **Patrik Andersson,**
the Swedish defender, turns down a move to Leeds

“Three weeks before kick-off I had eight players and a 15-stone goalkeeper who insisted he had done pre-season training.”
– **Alex Ferguson,**
on his first week in football management with East Stirling

“I’m not giving secrets like that to Milan. If I had my way I wouldn’t even tell them the time of the bloody kick-off.”
– **Bill Shankly,**
asked if he would name his team for that night’s European Cup tie

“I only hope it’s someone else’s body with *his* face painted on.”
– **Dino Zoff,**
the Lazio manager, after seeing pictures of a severely out of condition Paul Gascoigne

“Work-rate? That was never in my vocabulary when I was playing. You’re talking to the bloke who used to steal lifts on the milkman’s float during cross country runs.”
– **Jimmy Greaves**

“They've been loyal to me, and I can't question their honesty. When I came here they said there would be no money, and they've kept their promise.”

– **Dave Bassett,**
on the Sheffield United directors

“If I had the choice of a night out with Raquel Welch or going to the betting shop, I'd choose the betting shop every time.”

– **Stan Bowles,**
gets his priorities right

“I'm beginning to wonder what bloody vegetable grows in Norway.”

– **Graham Taylor,**
after the 'Turnip' and 'Onionhead' newspaper headlines

“Do you know the three most used words in football? 'Halifax Town nil.'”

– **John McGrath,**
Halifax manager

“The FA Cup Final is a great occasion, but only until ten minutes to three o'clock. Then the players come on and ruin the whole thing.”

– the late, great **Danny Blanchflower**

“Many of the world's great entertainers have changed in those Palladium dressing-rooms, but I was disappointed by them. They put me in mind of the dressing-rooms at Hartlepool.”

– **Chris Waddle,**
talking after his appearance with Glenn Hoddle on 'Live at the Palladium'

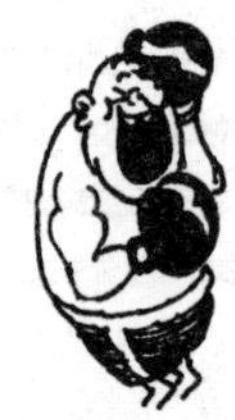

“When you’re as great as I am, it’s hard to be humble.”

– **Muhammad Ali,**
The Greatest

“I must have been three when I was born.”

– **Archie Moore,**
disagreeing with his mother on the year of his birth

“I fought Sugar Ray Robinson so many times it’s a wonder I didn’t get diabetes.”

– **Jake La Motta**
The Raging Bull

“I lost by default, not by de punch.”

– **John Conteh,**
after he was stripped of his WBC light-heavyweight title

“A lot of boxing promoters couldn’t match the cheeks of their buttocks.”

– **Mickey Duff,**
boxing promoter

“He hit me and knocked me face down on the canvas. I was in the land of make-believe. I heard saxophones and trombones. I saw little blue rats, and they were all smoking cigars and drinking whisky.”

– **James ‘Quick’ Tillis,**
heavyweight, on being knocked down by Earnie Shavers

"The bell went ding and I went dong!"

– **Lloyd Honeyghan,**
on his knockdown of Johnny Bumphus with the first punch of round two of his world title defence

"I was once knocked out by a Mexican bantamweight – six of my pals were swinging him around by his heels at the time."

– **Randall 'Tex' Cobb,**
heavyweight hardman

"They all look better than Rocky when they're doing their job and boxing. But they don't look so good when they're on the canvas."

– **Charlie Goldman,**
Rocky Marciano's trainer

"The ego has landed!"

– **Reg Gutteridge,**
ITV's voice of boxing, after one of Chris Eubank's rope-vaulting ring entrances

"I was never knocked out. I've been unconscious, but it's always been on my feet."

– **Floyd Patterson,**
the first man to regain the world heavyweight title

"We're all endowed with certain God-given talents. Mine happens to be punching people in the head."

– **Sugar Ray Leonard**

"Shakespeare? What weight is he?"

– **Harry Greb**
middleweight legend

"Brian London possesses the most unbeautiful face – it looks as if it fell apart and was re-assembled by a drunken mechanic."

– **Michael Parkinson**
broadcaster and writer

"There's more tension in golf than in boxing because golfers bring it on themselves. It's silly really because it's not as if the golf ball is going to jump up and belt you on the whiskers, is it?"

– **Henry Cooper**

"When I was a kid, we only stole things that began with an A – A fridge, A car, A watch..."

– **Rocky Graziano**

"I had the bravest manager in the world. He didn't care who I fought."

– **Willie Pep**
world featherweight champion

"Sugar Ray Leonard's retirements last about as long as Elizabeth Taylor's marriages."

– **Bob Arum,**
American promoter

"Intellectually, I went into jail with a peashooter and came out armed with a nuclear bomb. I made time serve me, rather than me serve time."

– **Don King**

"The ring – that's where I conduct my business. And my business is beating up people."

– **Thomas Hearns**

“Jim Watt is the perfect professional. Mind you, he wouldn't win any body-building prizes. He looks like a bottle of milk with gloves on.”

– **Terry Lawless,**
master manager, on Jim Watt, one of four boxers he guided to world titles

“Herol boxed just like a horse that has been nobbled.”

– **Barney Eastwood,**
manager and bookmaker after Herol Graham's defeat in a European title fight

“You always say 'I'll definitely quit when I start to slide,' and then one morning you wake up and realise you've done slid.”

– **Sugar Ray Robinson,**
the legend, on when to call it a day

“It pays me better to knock out teeth than to put them in.”

– **Frank Moran,**
heavyweight, asked why he gave up dentistry to take up boxing

“You know fellas, I don't think the kid's all there. I think he's scrambled in the marbles.”

– **Sonny Liston,**
on Cassius Clay

“Sonny Liston's so ugly that when he cries the tears run down the back of his head.”

– **Cassius Clay**

“Joe Frazier's so ugly, they ought to donate his face to the World Wildlife Fund.”

– **Muhammad Ali**

“Cassius Clay can’t insult me. I’m too ignorant.”

– **Brian London**

“If they said I had to defend my title against Mahatma Gandhi, I would fight him.”

– **Barry McGuigan,**
ready to take on allcomers

“Putting a fighter in the business world is like putting silk stockings on a pig.”

– **Jack Hurley**
American manager

“Boxers are only prawns in this game.”

– **Joe Bugner**

“I was called ‘Rembrandt’ Hope in my boxing days, because I spent so much time on the canvas.”

– **Bob Hope**

“I know it’s said that I can’t punch, but you should see me putting the cat out at night.”

– **Chris Finnegan**

“Herol Graham has turned defensive boxing into a poetic art. Trouble is, nobody ever knocked anyone out with a poem.”

– **Eddie Shaw,**
trainer, on Herol Graham

“It’s gonna be a thriller, a chiller and a killer ... when I get the gorilla in Manila.”

– **Muhammad Ali,**
before his third fight with Joe Frazier

"That guy's so dumb, he can't take a shower and sing at the same time."

– **Chubb Feeny,**
American football executive on one of his team

"There's this lineman who's as big as a gorilla and as strong as a gorilla. If only he was as smart as a gorilla we'd have a real find."

– **Sam Bailey,**
American football coach on a young prospect

"There's nothing wrong with Gerry Ford except he played football too long without his helmet."

– **Lyndon B. Johnson,**
referring to one of his successors as President

"My Premier advised me that as I was about to squeeze the trigger I should imagine I was shooting at the enemies of my country."

– **Ho Jun Li,**
North Korea's small-bore rifle gold medallist at the 1972 Munich Olympics

"I played like a slow puncture."

– **John Parrott,**
on his losing performance in the 1989 Embassy World Snooker final

“Mention that you are a hammer thrower to someone who is not an athletics enthusiast and you will be met with any reaction from a puzzled frown to raucous laughter. If you have the misfortune to say it to a groundsman, you may face physical violence.”

– **Howard Payne,**
hammer thrower

“I swing big, with everything I got. I hit big or I miss big. I like to live as big as I can.”

– **Babe Ruth,**
baseball great

“There are two things no man will admit he can't do well – drive and make love.”

– **Stirling Moss,**
motor racing ace

“Sometimes I have to give away the cups I win, because I don't have room for them in my luggage.”

– **Althea Gibson,**
American tennis legend

“When Nastase is winning he's objectionable. When he's losing he's highly objectionable.”

– **Adrian Clark,**
tennis linesman, on Ilie Nastase, the volatile Romanian

“We've lost seven of our last eight matches. The only team we have beaten is Western Samoa. It's a good job we didn't play the whole of Samoa.”

– **Gareth Davies,**
Welsh Rugby Union player, on his country's decline at international level after the glory years

"You decide you'll wait for your pitch, then, as the ball starts towards the plate you think about your stance, and then you think about your swing, and then you realise that what went past you for a strike was your pitch."

– **Bobby Mercer,**
baseball star, on his loss of form

"Give Chris a finger like I did and she'll take the whole hand."

– **Eva Pfaff,**
tennis player, following a defeat by Chris Evert

"Ninety per cent of baseball is half mental."

– **Jim Wohlford,**
baseball player

"Billiards is very similar to snooker, except there are only three balls and no one watches it."

– **Steve 'Interesting' Davis**

"All my life I've been naturally quick and am used to running on my toes. Now I often feel as if I'm on my bloody knees."

– **Steve Ovett**

"New Yorkers love it when you spill your guts out there. Spill your guts at Wimbledon and they make you stop and clean it up."

– **Jimmy Connors**

"I deserved to get run over – but Steve didn't just knock me down. He backed over me a couple of times to make sure."

– **Kirk Stevens,**
following a snooker defeat by Steve Longworth

“I couldn’t have done it without my bowling bowl.”
– **Millie Ignizio,**
American ten-pin bowling champion

“Frankly, I’d rather have a drink with Idi Amin.”
– **Alex Higgins,**
on Steve Davis

“Quarterbacks? They’re just human people.”
– **Art Rooney,**
American football team owner

“I always say that to maintain an interest in sport, it is important never to meet sportsmen.”
– **Roy Hattersley**

“I always say that to maintain an interest in politics, it is important not to meet politicians.”
– **Jimmy Greaves**
reacting to the quote from Roy Hattersley

“They say Steve Cauthen is 18 and comes from Bluegrass country, but I don’t believe them – he’s 103 and comes from another planet.”
– **Laz Bazzera,**
American horse trainer

“Should’ve, would’ve, could’ve. It’s God’s way of torturing you when you lose.”
– **Brad Gilbert,**
American tennis player

“I don’t talk to horses, but I do try to humour them if they don’t want to go.”
– **Lester Piggott**

"I haven't felt like this since my uncle's funeral in 1986. We were in the cemetery when somebody got the score from the Arms Park: Wales 15, France 23. It cast a gloom over the whole proceedings."

– **Max Boyce,**
Welsh comedian, on hearing of Wales' 63-6 Rugby Union defeat by Australia

"I not speak the English so good, but then I speak the driving well."

– **Emerson Fittipaldi,**
Brazilian motor racing ace

"I'm at that difficult age where I'm physically unable to compete, but mentally too alert to become a selector."

– **Sebastian Coe,**
considers his future in 1987

"I don't want to be disrespectful to my fellow snooker players, but it is a joke how I keep losing to so many mugs."

– **Jimmy White**

"One critic wrote that the only thing more wooden on the stage was the tree."

– **Ian Botham,**
discussing his notices after his pantomime debut

“He doesn’t know the meaning of the word fear. Of course, there are lots of other words he doesn’t know the meaning of either.”

– **Sid Gillman,**
American football coach, on one of his players

“Playing in the second row doesn’t require a lot of intelligence really. You’ve got to be bloody crazy to play there for a start.”

– **Bill Beaumont**

“I have been described as fat, boozy and toothless. That’s pretty accurate, I guess.”

– **Jocky Wilson,**

“Pat Cash is wrong to claim he is the first Australian to win at Wimbledon while wearing a diamond earring. What about Evonne Cawley?”

– **Jimmy Greaves**

“English football has become a grey game, played by grey players, run by grey people and watched by grey crowds in grey stadiums.”

– **Rodney Marsh**
before leaving Fulham to play and coach in the United States

“We went to the end of the world, turned left at Australia and there it was.”

– **Bob Hiller**
the England Rugby international’s reply on his return from a Lions tour when asked how he had found New Zealand

And, finally, in this *Hark Who's Talking* chapter, here is a collection of things they wish they hadn't said on television ...

"For the benefit of those of you watching in black and white, Spurs are wearing the yellow shirts."
– John Motson

"In the rear, the small diminutive figure of Shoaib Mohammad, who can't be much taller or shorter than he is."
– Henry Blofeld,
cricket commentator

"It's Oxford! No, it's Cambridge! It's difficult to see. It's Oxford ... no ... well, one of them must be winning!"
– John Snagge,
BBC radio commentator at the 1954 Boat Race

"Charlie George has just pissed a late fartness test."
– Bob Wilson
in his first trial run in front of a BBC TV camera

"There's a fly ball to deep centre field. Winfield is going back, back. He hits his head against the wall. It's rolling back towards second base."
– Jerry Coleman,
baseball commentator

“This could be a repeat of what will happen next week at the European championships.”

– **David Coleman**

“Believe it or not, goals can change a game.”

– **Mike Channon**

“Paul Azinger is wearing an all black outfit – black jumper, blue trousers, white shoes and a pink tea cosy.”

– **Renton Laidlaw,**
golf commentator

“A mediocre season for Nelson Piquet as he is now known and always has been.”

– **Murray Walker**

“I am speaking from a deserted and virtually empty Crucible Theatre.”

– **David Vine**

“The players with the wind will have to control it a lot more.”

– **Jack Charlton**

“He's going for the pink – and for those of you with black and white sets, the yellow is behind the blue.”

– **'Whispering' Ted Lowe,**
snooker commentator

“He's a very competitive competitor, that's the sort of competitor he is.”

– **Dorian Williams,**
late master show jumping commentator

"It's a battle with himself and with the ticking finger of the clock."

– **David Coleman**

"If you didn't know him, you wouldn't know who he was."

– **Nigel Starmer-Smith,**
Rugby Union commentator

"There is Johan Cruyff, who at 35 has added a whole new meaning to the word Anno Domini."

– **Archie MacPherson**

"In technical terms, he's making a real pig's ear of it."

– **Peter Alliss,**
golf commentator

"Greg Lemond has literally come back from the dead to lead the Tour de France."

– **Phil Liggett,**
cycling commentator

"He has got perfect control over the ball right up to the moment he lets it go."

– **Peter Walker,**
cricket commentator

"When the stalls open, the horses are literally going to explode."

– **Brough Scott**

"With half the race gone, there is still half the race to go."

– **Murray Walker**

"Ian Rush unleashed his left foot and it hit the back of the net."

– **Mike England**

"If you hadn't been there it wouldn't have been much of a fight."

– **Harry Carpenter,**
interviewing Ken Norton after his controversial points loss to Muhammad Ali

"People started calling me 'Fiery' because 'Fiery' rhymes with Fred just like 'Typhoon' rhymes with Tyson."

– **Fred Trueman**

"After a goalless first-half, the score at half-time is 0-0."

– **Brian Moore**

"He must have discovered euthanasia – he never seems to get any older."

– **Johnny Francome,**
jockey

"You know the Brazilians aren't as good as they used to be, or as they are now."

– **Kenny Dalglish**

"He used to be fairly indecisive, but now he's not so certain."

– **Peter Alliss**

"The Austrians are wearing the dark black socks."

– **Barry Davies**

"He certainly handed out more than he gave."

– **Harry Carpenter**

"The Argentinians are numbered alphabetically."

– **John Motson**

"The pendulum is swinging back and forth like a metronome."

– **Sid Waddell,**
darts commentator

"He won the bronze medal in the 1976 Olympics, so he's used to being out in front."

– **David Coleman**

"That was a delightful bit of play by Madonna."

– **Archie McPherson,**
describing a goal by Maradona in the 1994 World Cup

"Asa Hartford is giving a whole-hearted performance."

– **David Coleman,**
a few days after footballer Asa Hartford had been told he had a hole in his heart

"With the very last kick of the game, Macdonald has scored with a header."

– **Alan Parry**

"From the way Denny's shaking his head, he's either got an injured shoulder or a gnat in his eye."

– **Jerry Coleman,**
baseball commentator

"He would have potted that ball ninety-nine times out of a thousand."

– **Ted Lowe**

"Paul Allott is the lovely type of chap you want to meet behind the pavilion."

– **Henry Blofeld**

5: Tales of the Unexpected

Finally, just for a sporting laugh, here is a jamboree of stories with a sting in the tale.

Full-backs Bob Hiller and JPR Williams were drafted in as makeshift forwards during a training session on the 1971 Lions tour of New Zealand. They packed down against Scotland's dynamic prop forward Ian 'Mighty Mouse' McLauchlan, a notorious joker. During one scrum Hiller suddenly gave out a yelp and jumped up holding his ear where McLauchlan had taken a nibble. JPR was heard to mutter, 'He'd better not try that on me.' Mighty Mouse either didn't hear or didn't heed the warning. During the next scrum down he fastened his teeth on JPR's ear, and the next thing he knew he was lying flat on his back. JPR had reacted to the bite with a swinging right to the jaw. 'That,' said JPR to the amusement of everybody but the dazed McLauchlan, 'proves that my bark is worse than your bite.'

Liverpool were the visitors to Queen's Park Rangers where a centre-forward called Frank Saul (a goal-scoring hero for Spurs in the 1967 FA Cup Final) was having a bit of a nightmare. In the second half a dog came scampering on to the pitch and the game was held up while players and officials chased the intruder. The chase was still in progress when a loud Cockney voice boomed from the terraces, 'Leave the dog on – take Saul off.'

Andy Williams, the singer who is a golf fanatic, was having one of those rounds when nothing would go right during a charity tournament in Atlanta. He was continually in and out of the woods, spent more time in the bunker than Hitler and rarely saw the fairway. On reaching the 18th green he asked his caddie: 'What should I do with this putt?' The caddie advised: 'Keep it as low as possible.'

When West Ham United won the FA Cup in 1964 I went with manager Ron Greenwood to a charity lunch in London's West End on the Monday after the victory over Preston. Ron took the FA Cup with him, and for the first time in its history the famous trophy travelled by tube. I took the train ride with Ron, and he gave me the privilege of carrying the Cup, which was hidden inside a red cloth bag. 'If anybody asks you what's in the bag,' Ron said, 'tell them, "Sweet FA."'

My old mate Peter Osgood went one better with the FA Cup. He slept with it! Peter took the Cup home with him after helping Southampton beat Manchester United in the 1976 Final, and cuddled up with the trophy in bed.

It was the final after-match banquet of a Scotland Rugby tour of Argentina that had been scarred by brawls and stiff-armed tackles, with the Argentinians as the perpetrators. Jim Telfer, Scotland's captain who was noted for his forthright views, stood up and made a no-punches-pulled speech. 'If you wish to be accepted internationally you must cut out the dirty play,' he said. 'In all my time in the game I have never come up against opposition so set on intimidatory tactics.' Jim sat down and let the interpreter translate his tough words into Spanish. The interpretation of his five-minute speech lasted just 20 seconds. When the interpreter sat down, Jim asked him what he had said. 'I thought it best just to use that bit about what a beautiful country this is,' he replied. 'I did not wish to risk an international incident!'

During a match at Anfield, Liverpool lion Tommy Smith,

he of the thunderous tackle, was having a verbal battle with Coventry City forward Tommy Hutchison, he of the winged feet. Hutch decided on a novel way to settle their argument.

'Tell you what, Smithie,' he said. 'I'll race you to the half-way line for your wages.'

The Anfield Iron Man knew that strength rather than speed was his ace. 'You're on,' he said. 'But only if we can then have a double-or-nothing wager on a scrap afterwards.'

Hutch politely declined.

I was at Marylebone register office on the Saturday morning in 1967 when George Graham was married, with Terry Venables as his best man. Four hours later they played against each other at Highbury, Graham for Arsenal and Venables for Tottenham. The Gunners gave Spurs a 4-0 hiding, and joker Venables said at the wedding party: 'As the fourth goal went in, George strolled over to me and said, "It's me who should be saving myself for tonight, not you!"'

If you're an animal lover you may want to skip this true story. Eddie Clamp, Jon Sammels and John McLeod, Arsenal clubmates in the 1960s, were invited to join in a 'shoot' by a wealthy Highbury supporter who had his own country estate. The players were armed with 12-bore shotguns and spent two frustrating hours without getting a single sight of a bird or rabbit. They were just about to give up and go home when Eddie Clamp was alerted by a rustling sound in a hedge. He blasted off with both barrels and the rustling stopped. When he went to see what he had bagged, he found he had shot the estate owner's dog.

Charlie Williams was a good-class professional footballer before he found fame as one of *The Comedians*. In his rich Yorkshire accent, he tells this story of his days as a powerful centre-half with Doncaster Rovers when he was one of only a handful of black players in the League:

'Several times when playing down in t'south I heard the shout from the terraces, "Get back to your own country, you big black bastard." Ee, I 'ad to laugh. It were only two pounds on train back t'Barnsley.

'Don't you believe those stories that when I made my debut for t'Rovers I picked up t'brown ball and shook it to see if there were any milk in it.

'I remember a game I played for Rovers against Middlesbrough. I was marking their young centre-forward. Brian Clough were his name, and he'd been proving too much of a handful for every defence. I prided myself on being one of those footballers who couldn't play t'game, but by heck could I stop others from playing it! I stuck that close to Cloughie that he said, "If I go for a piss will you follow me?"

'I told him, "I won't follow thee, lad, but I'll be waiting here for thee when tha comes back!"'

Seconds out for a true story from Paddy Byrne, boxing's man of many talents who in a 40-year career in the professional game has been manager, matchmaker, trainer, cornerman, agent and cuts man: 'I took a boxer to Denmark for an eight-round contest. We flew from London to Copenhagen, a flight that took little more than an hour. I thought my boxer was in good shape and could not understand why he was puffing and blowing after just three rounds.

'As he flopped down on his stool at the end of the third, I asked, "What's wrong with you?"

'He shrugged his shoulders and said with deadly seriousness, "I must be suffering from jet lag."'

This brings me to a true Irish story about Pat Desmond,

a heavyweight boxer who had the gift of the gab as well as the jab. Desmond was taking a hammering in an All-Ireland heavyweight championship contest and went down on his knees in his own corner early in the second round. His second shouted, 'Don't get up till nine, Pat ... Don't get up till nine.' Still kneeling, Pat shouted back: 'And what time is it now?'

Rugged Birmingham City defender Gary Pendrey sent an opponent crashing with a late tackle in a League match at St Andrews. The referee ran after him and warned, 'Do that again and you're off.'

'What was the matter with it, ref?' asked Pendrey, spreading his arms in a gesture of innocence.

You know you were late,' snapped the ref.

'But I got there as fast as I could,' said Pendrey.

Raconteur Tony O'Reilly, whose Rugby career with Ireland was one long sporting laugh, gives this lovely taste of the build-up to an England-Ireland match at Twickenham in the 1950s: 'We were always devising plans to reduce England's home advantage at Twickenham. One I remember was sending a mis-shapen Irish forward with a Rugby ball stuck up the back of his jersey to make him look like Quasimodo, into the England dressing-room. We timed it so that he arrived at what we knew would be the peak moment of a call to arms by their skipper Eric Evans.

'Just as Eric was giving his final harangue – "Remember Waterloo" (with an Irish-born captain, incidentally), and "Remember Alamein" (with another) – our man pushed open the door and said, "Sorry to be disturbing you, lads, but would any of you be having some hairy twine I could be borrowing for me boots?" It didn't help us win the match, but it provided us with a laugh. And that's surely what the game and life should be about it.'

I caught wind of a story that caused quite a stink at the Fartown ground of Rugby League club Huddersfield where that great character Alex Murphy was the coach. Alex was a member of a syndicate that paid £10,000 for a National Hunt racehorse. They applied to the Jockey Club to have the horse registered under the name of Fartowner – as in far towner. The stewards of the Jockey Club turned up their noses at this, claiming that the name was 'not considered suitable'. So the syndicate settled for the name Claret and Gold, Huddersfield's colours. The radio and television horse racing commentators were relieved the Fartowner was not accepted. They still have pronunciation problems with a horse glorying in the name of Hoof Hearted!

Comedian Tommy Trinder was one of football's outstanding personalities when he was chairman of Fulham. He once walked into the dressing-room at Craven Cottage to find trainer Frank Penn massaging a greyhound.

'What's that?' asked Tommy. 'Our new centre-forward?'

'It's a greyhound,' said the trainer.

'I can see that,' said Tommy. 'But what's it doing here?'

'It belongs to Charlie Mitten,' (then Fulham's outside-left) explained Frank. 'We're getting it in the mood for tonight's big race.'

Charlie Mitten came in at that point. 'There you are, guv'nor,' said Charlie. 'Been looking for you to tell you about the dog.'

'Oh, that's most co-operative of you to tell me that we've given a bloody greyhound the run of Craven Cottage,' said Tommy, who was accustomed to Charlie's ducking and diving.

'Do yourself a favour, guv'nor, and get your pound notes on it,' said cheeky Charlie. 'It's running at Slough tonight and it's a racing certainty to finish first.'

'But you can't train greyhounds here,' protested Tommy. 'This is a football club. Well, that's what I like to believe.'

'I think you'll have to turn a blind eye just this once,' said Charlie, famous for his persuasive tongue. 'All the players have got their money on it, and it will upset them if we upset the dog.'

Tommy knew when he was beaten. He shrugged and handed Charlie a white fiver. 'Here,' he said, 'put this on for me when you go to the track.'

The dog trailed in last.

George Biddles was one of the most successful post-war boxing managers. George, who passed on after steering Richard Dunn to a world heavyweight title challenge against Muhammad Ali, told me of an early experience he had at his local arena in Leicester, Granby Halls: 'Two heavyweights were swinging away when a wayward punch landed on the referee's chin and knocked him face first to the canvas. He was groggy when he got up and was in no condition to continue. The substitute referee came bounding up the corner steps, tripped and twisted an ankle.

'It was the last contest on the bill, and it looked as if the fight would have to be abandoned. I had done some refereeing in the gymnasium and volunteered to take over to save the show. Within seconds of me shouting "box on" one of the heavyweights landed a knock-out punch. All I had to do was count to ten. I claim the shortest refereeing career in boxing history!'

Mickey Fox was a popular London boxing referee either side of the Second World War. He was officiating at a contest between an Englishman and a German before the war when the English boxer landed a knockdown blow. Mickey dropped on one knee alongside the stricken German fighter and started confidently shouting out the count in Deutsch, 'Einz, zwei, drei, vier, uh ...'

Suddenly Mickey's German vocabulary deserted him, and he continued: ' ... five, six, seven, eight, nine ...'

Then he remembered one more German word that the flattened boxer would prefer not to have heard, ' ... aus!'

Gary Sprake, Leeds and Wales goalkeeper, usually had a safe pair of hands, but when he made his mistakes it always seemed to be in front of the television cameras. His most infamous calamity came in a crucial match against Liverpool at Anfield. This is how his skipper at the time, Billy Bremner, remembered it: 'I recall that it was a horrible day. There was snow on the ground, it was freezing cold, and to add to our misery, we were losing what was a vital championship game.

'The match was into the second-half and we were trying to battle our way back into it when a harmless ball was knocked through to Gary Sprake. As he bent to pick it up we all started to move away down the field ready to start a counter-attack. As I approached the centre circle the ground erupted with a great roar from the Kop end behind our goal. I turned back to see Sprake standing on the edge of the eighteen-yard box with his hands covering his face.

'I looked in panic for the ball and there it was, nestling in the back of our net. All we Leeds players stood staring open mouthed, wondering what the hell had happened. I was standing near big Jack Charlton and referee Jim Finney. Jack and I looked at each other in sheer disbelief.

'Jack politely inquired of the referee what had occurred. Well, not quite like that. But you know what I mean. "What the blankety-blank's happened?' he asked.

'Jim Finney said in a matter-of-fact way: "Your goalkeeper has just thrown the ball into his own net."

'Now it was the turn of Big Jack and me to hold our heads in our hands. "What decision are you going to give, Jim?" Jack said.

'The ref, who was one of the game's great characters as well as a very respected referee, shrugged and smiled. "I've never come across this before," he said. "But I guess it will have to be a goal."

'And with that, he pointed very deliberately to the centre spot. Not one of us had seen the ball go into the net, but in that moment of confusion the three of us saw the funny side of it and started to laugh. We just fell about when the Kop choir, quick as a flash, started to sing the Des O'Connor hit song of that time, *Careless Hands.*'

I have usually identified the main characters in each of my stories, but in the following tales of the unexpected I protect the guilty and the innocent ... just in case they try to sue me (mind you, I would get them laughed out of court!):

There was a club cricketer who made headlines in the summer of 1991 when he was caught out with his girlfriend in the nearby woods when he was due in to bat. This story would have revived memories for a famous Test bowler who was once discovered bowling a maiden over in the dressing-room long after the close of play.

'I'm shutting up now, sir,' announced an embarrassed groundsman.

The England star would have us believe that he replied, 'I wish you would shut up. Tha's putting me off my line and length.'

A former Test batsman told me this story on the understanding that I would protect his identity: 'I was fielding on the boundary during a County match when I caught the eye of a beautiful girl sitting a couple of rows back. We exchanged smiles and I wondered how I could ask her for a date.

'As luck would have it, a boy came up and asked me for my autograph, pushing a piece of paper and a pencil into my hand. I signed my name, and then I wrote my telephone number on the bottom of the paper and tore it off.

'A couple of overs later I was delighted to see the ball sailing over my head for a six. As I retrieved it I pushed the piece of paper with the telephone number into the girl's hand.

'There is not a happy ending. It turned out she was the fiancee of the man who hit the six!'

A County cricketer – an opening batsman – walked with his bride through an archway of cricket bats following their wedding. He received a roar of laughter during his speech at the reception when he said, 'My wife has asked me what my team-mates would have held up if I had been a bowler!'

I am assured that the following story is true, but I have my doubts: The professional of a Surrey golf club was giving a male club member a lesson when two women golfers walked off the eighteenth green at the end of a round. 'Crikey, there's my wife with my bit on the side,' said the pro. The man having a lesson looked up, watched the two walking away and said, 'No, that's *my* wife with *my* bit on the side.'

It is a former Welsh international who told me this mind-blowing story: 'The Welsh squad for a 1960s international match in East Germany gathered at London Airport. There were ten officials, manager Dave Bowen, trainer Jack Jones, eight pressmen and *ten* players. It was the usual old story that some clubs were not releasing their players until the last minute, and it had been arranged for two other players to join us the next day just a few hours before the kick-off.

'Anyway, our flight was called and there was the usual panic rush from the duty-free shop to the departure gate. There was quite a bit of jockeying and jostling as we filed on to the plane; you know, with players trying to get with mates and Welsh officials getting as far away from us as possible. This, of course, was in the days before you were allocated a specific seat.

'Finally we were all seated with the exception of one FA councillor who was standing in the aisle looking lost. The flight had been overbooked by one. After several minutes the air hostess announced that the last person named on the checking-in list would have to leave the plane and catch a later flight. As we were going to East Germany in the cold war era, these flights were not exactly every five minutes. She read out the last name: 'Mr G.Reece. Would Mr G. Reece kindly leave the aircraft.' This, of course, was Gil Reece, one of our ten players. There was a long silence as we all waited for one of the officials to surrender his place so that Gil could stay on board. A couple of them fidgeted uncomfortably in their seats and the man standing in the aisle tried to make himself invisible. Nobody moved.

'Eventually, with a gesture of disgust and disbelief, Gil got up and walked off the plane. The rest of us, who had been picked to represent our country in a prestige international, didn't know whether to laugh or cry as we took off with nine players.

'After the flight had been under way for about half an hour, one of the Welsh Football Association officials approached the pressmen who were sitting just behind me at the rear of the plane. They were expecting an explanation or perhaps even an admission that the officials had been wrong to leave Gil Reece behind. They leaned forward, notebooks at the ready.

'I feel it only right that I should mention this, boys,' he

said. 'I thought one of you might have had the decency to volunteer to stay behind ...'

On a later Welsh trip, Newcastle goalkeeper Dave Hollins – brother of Chelsea's John Hollins – joined the squad at the airport for an international match in Greece. He was wearing his Newcastle club blazer.

In the bus taking them from the departure lounge to the aircraft, Dave stood next to a Welsh FA selector who took a close interest in the badge on Dave's blazer. 'What badge is that?' he asked.

'Newcastle United,' said Dave.

'Really,' said the old boy. 'Where are you off to, then?'

'Greece, of course,' replied Dave, trying not to look too puzzled.

'What a coincidence,' the official beamed. 'So are we ...'

One old boy who was a big noise in the Football League and the Football Association used to butcher the English language. He was chairman of a disciplinary committee and told the player standing before him, 'I can promise you a pathetic hearing.'

After a crowd riot at his club, he made a plea 'for sanitary to be restored to the game'.

Another of his classic gaffes was to say at an after-match banquet, 'I would like to thank our Bulgarian hosts for their wonderful hospitality.' The England squad were in Romania at the time.

And he was the same man who during an England tour of Latin America stood on the beach in the millionaires' paradise of Acapulco and – thumbs tugging his braces – said in all seriousness, 'Give me Blackpool any day.'

An English punter who drowned his sorrows after losing his money on Generous in the 1991 Arc de Triomphe at Langchamp was helped aboard a London-bound charter-flight in a legless condition. It was only when he started to sober up somewhere over the white cliffs of Dover that he realised he had motored to Paris.

An old friend, Jack Kerslake, of Scarborough, passed on this golfing story: 'I arranged a game at our local club with my father, who was well into his eighties and becoming somewhat absent-minded. We were off to a good start to the day when we went to the boot of the car to find that instead of packing his golf clubs he had put in a bag of gardening tools!

'We hired a set of clubs and then started our round. On the first tee Dad sliced the ball into the woods on the right. I went off to take my second shot and then walked back to help him find his ball. When I reached the woods he was nowhere to be seen.

'I waved through the following four-ball and then hurried back to the clubhouse to see if Dad was there. There was no sign of him, and as I returned in panic towards the first fairway I caught sight of him. He was preparing to putt on the eighteenth green!

'He had come out of the woods on the other side where the eighteenth fairway runs parallel with the first. "What kept you?" he asked. "Did you lose your ball?"

'I could not talk for laughing. He had completed the course in four shots!'

This is what is known as an 'under-pa' story.

I am indebted to Anne Shacklock, of Onchan, Isle of Man, for this classic golf story: 'My husband was trying to persuade me to take up the game, and one afternoon he talked me into walking round the course with him. Four women were preparing to leave the first tee after driving off as we arrived.

'They proceeded down the fairway chatting merrily and after about 60 yards the first woman took her second shot. Within the next few yards, two more women took their second shots. The fourth member appeared to be searching for something, then had a conversation with her friends.

'She then started to walk back towards the tee, hauling her trolley. My husband said, "Lost your ball, Mrs-so-and-so?"

'"Oh no," she replied, reaching into her bag for a ball. "I've just realised that I forgot to drive."

'Watching these women convinced me I could not possibly do worse and they were enjoying it so. I have since had years of pleasure playing the wonderful game.'

I am such an atrocious golfer that my friends call me Roger Rabbit. I have to confess that I once played a first hole without a ball. I mimed every shot rather than risk making fool of myself as golfers queued behind. My partner was single-handicapped Roy Ullyett, the peerless *Daily Express* sports cartoonist, who always draws a good crowd. As we reached the green, he said: 'I'll give you that putt.'

I had the sheer pleasure of working in harness with the comedy master Eric Morecambe for six years on a series of 'Sports-smile' columns for the *Daily Express* and the *Titbits* magazine. Eric, a Luton Town director, told me this story that had been passed on to him by the director of a visiting League club: 'The club chairman went home unexpectedly early one day and caught his wife in bed with the club's star centre-forward. Now the chairman had a real dilemma on his hands.

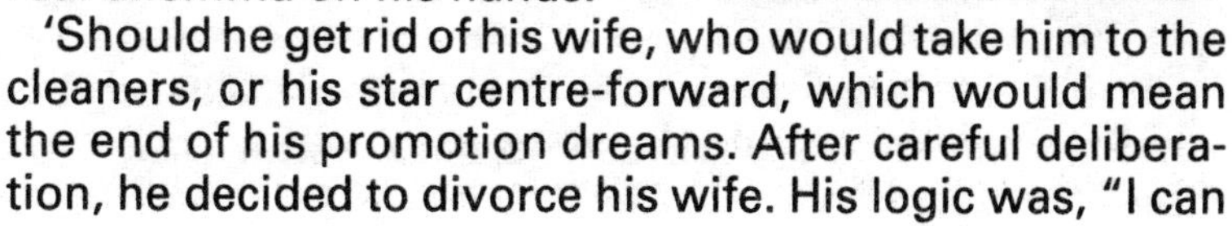

'Should he get rid of his wife, who would take him to the cleaners, or his star centre-forward, which would mean the end of his promotion dreams. After careful deliberation, he decided to divorce his wife. His logic was, "I can always get myself another wife, but where would I find another centre-forward with a left foot like my star player?"'

At this point Eric put his glasses to an acute angle on his face as he added, 'The centre-forward won it by a foot. Now there's a novelty!'

Here's a cricket story that could have come out of the Basil Fawlty Comedy Academy. It is told by a schoolteacher acquaintance of mine, Harrison Shaw: 'In my early days as a teacher in London's East End I was put in charge of the cricket team for a match against a posh school in Esher.

'I shared the umpiring duties with the Esher teacher, a John Cleese lookalike and a crusty man of little patience.

'One of my lads was an exceptionally fast bowler, but he could not get his run-up right. After no-balling him four times in as many balls, the Cleese character bellowed to me at square leg, "Tell this stupid boy to let the ball go earlier ..."

'Our captain advised him to release the ball before reaching the crease, but he over-reacted, let the ball go two yards before the crease, and it clunked my fellow umpire on the head.

'As he fell to his knees in a daze, he managed to announce with a strangled voice, "No ball". We spent the rest of the innings with spinners operating from each end.'

This reminds me of a story from my old friend Tom Graveney, one of the most elegant batsman ever to wield the willow. He told me how he once found the umpire sitting with the members as he went into bat in a County match. 'What are you doing there?' asked Tom. 'Shouldn't you be in the middle?'

'The way this lot barracked my last lbw decision,' the umpire replied, 'it's obvious you get a better view from here.'

Club Rugby player John Curtis, of Weymouth, told me this tale of the unexpected: 'Our club ground is surrounded by houses, and there is one old boy, who lives directly behind the posts, who gets angry every time the ball lands in his garden.

'One afternoon he was up a ladder painting the outside of his house when I put over a high conversion, and the ball thudded against the wall that he was painting.

'When I asked the age-old question, "Please can we have our ball back?", he growled, "You nearly had me off my ladder. Here's your bloody ball."

'What arrived in my hands from the other side of the fence was a newly whitewashed ball. He had deliberately dropped it into his bucket of paint!'

Back in my football reporting days I once accompanied the then Colchester United manager Neil Franklin to a house adjoining the Layer Road ground to try to sweeten a local resident, who was refusing to return seven balls that had been kicked into his garden during League games.

Neil knocked at the door and an old chap who was hard of hearing opened it, cupping a hand to his ear as Neil loudly explained that we had come about the footballs in the garden.

His face suddenly lit up when he realised he had Neil Franklin, one of England's greatest ever centre-halves, on his doorstep, and he invited us in.

As Neil recounted his England playing experiences at the top of his voice, I sat wondering how I could break the news to him that we had knocked on the wrong door!

Snooker has always been a game that draws people with a gambling instinct. The next two stories illustrate the lengths to which some players will go to win their side bets:

Frank Heard, of Stoke-on-Trent, told me this tale: 'I called into a snooker hall for a game while visiting Birmingham and was hooked into having bets with an obvious hustler. He only started to produce his best play when the bet was

£50 a frame, and there were side bets being struck by spectators. I was into what seemed a match-winning break when suddenly a cat leapt on to the table and sent the balls scattering all over the place.

'"Game abandoned ... all bets off," announced the hustler. It was past midnight, and the hustler, who turned out to be the owner, insisted he had to close for the night.

'It was only later that I learned that the cat was a well-trained accomplice. If he was struggling, he would give the signal for the cat to be released from its basket, and it would always leap on to the table because that was where its food dish was placed during non-playing times.'

The cat arrived on cue, so to speak. It gives a whole new meaning to The Cat and the Fiddle!

My second hustler story is told by Martin Bignall, of Hythe in Kent: 'When I was mis-spending my youth at a snooker hall in Manchester the owner had a Doberman dog that he used to let off the leash if ever he was in trouble in a betting match. One night a friend of mine was into what looked a winning break when the dog came bounding towards him. He was so startled that his cue slipped and ripped a huge tear in the cloth on the table. The face of the snooker hall owner was a picture.'

He must have felt in need of a break.

Here's a boxing story from Frank Donaldson, of Cleethorpes, that really counted with a referee: 'I was volunteered for the Army regional boxing championships simply because I was a hefty bloke, and I found myself up against the best fighter in the Grenadier Guards. I was giving away three inches in height and more than a stone, and I was petrified.

'As the first bell rang I decided on hit or bust tactics, and I went out swinging with my eyes shut. I had the satisfaction of feeling my right fist make contact, and there was a roar from the crowd. As I opened my eyes I saw the referee on his way down to the canvas, out to the world.

'They had to use smelling salts to bring him round. I was too upset to continue and pulled out of the fight, and I have never been in the ring since.

'My opponent went on to bigger and better things. He was Jack Gardner, who became the British, Empire (as it was then) and European heavyweight champion.'

Former amateur referee Gerald Hopkins, of Porthcawl, tops that knock-out story. He told me this hilarious tale: 'I was refereeing a contest in Swansea between two novice amateur heavyweights who were swinging wildly. I had to side-step smartly to avoid being hit by one of them, and in so doing I stumbled into his opponent. My elbow landed in his eye, which immediately closed.

'I had to abandon the contest, and it gave a whole new meaning to "referee stops fight". Everybody thought it was funny except the poor chap I hit. When I got back into the ring for my next contest, a spectator shouted: "Watch out for the ref – he hits on the blindside."'

There have been scores of stories about legendary Liverpool manager Bill Shankly over the years. My favourite is the one that Alan Ball tells: 'I had been booked for a tackle on Liverpool's Ian Callaghan by referee Clive Thomas. Shanks told me afterwards that he didn't think the tackle warranted a booking, and he generously said that he would give evidence for me if I wanted to appeal. The hearing was in London, and Shanks came down with Chris Lawler who had to appear before the committee about another booking.

'Chris was first in and was found guilty, despite a plea on

his behalf by Shanks. Then it was my turn to be called before the committee. There was a game of table football set out on a board in front of the officials so that people involved could move the little plastic players to show what happened.

'First Clive Thomas and his two linesmen gave their version of what had happened. One of the linesmen had his evidence dismissed because the committee felt that he was too far away from where I had made the tackle.

'Then I gave evidence and called Ian Callaghan as my first witness. He said he thought that the tackle had been a fair one. Next I called Shanks. "Please describe the incident to us, Mr Shankly," said the committee chairman.

'"Certainly, sir," said Shanks in his Scottish growl of a voice. "But first I want to say that the referee in Chris Lawler's case was a bloody liar."

'The chairman moved uncomfortably in his seat. "Quite, Mr Shankly," he said. "But that case is closed. Can you please confine your comments to this case."

'Shanks gave one of those looks of his that could turn rock to jelly. Then he gave a full account of how he had been astonished to see the referee book me for an innocuous tackle. "It was perfectly fair in this man's game of ours and did not warrant a booking, just like Chris Lawler did not deserve to have his name taken."

'"Yes," said the chairman. "You have made your point about the Lawler case. Just how clearly did you see Ball's tackle?"

'"I saw it clearly from my position in the dug-out," said

Shanks. Clive Thomas jumped in with what he considered a relevant point. "You say you were sitting in the dug-out, Mr Shankly," he said. "Well I have to inform you that one of my linesmen has had his evidence dismissed because it was considered he was standing too far away from the incident. Yet he was standing on the touchline in front of the dug-out at the time. How could you possibly have seen what was happening if you were behind him?"

'The ref appeared to have made a good point in true Perry Mason fashion. But Shanks was never beaten that easily in his life.

'Back he came with the reply: "I saw the incident developing and so I stood up and threw the linesman to one side so that I could have an unobstructed view of what was about to happen."

'The whole room shook with laughter. This was Shanks at his most outrageous. What a character.'

As I promised in the introduction, I have kept a reasonably low profile. But now I need to come out in the open with some personal recollections that I hope will keep you amused. I have earned my daily bread nibbling around the edges of the sports world for the last forty years, and I close *This Sporting Laugh* with a few memories of newspaper colleagues who have brightened my path with their humour and companionship. My first Fleet Street tale of the unexpected revolves around Peter Corrigan, a former Sports Editor of the *Observer* and now a bitingly witty columnist with the *Independent on Sunday*. Peter and I were two of seven national daily reporters covering an England international football tour of Europe in the summer of 1967. Peter was then on the *Sun* and I was penning a living with the *Daily Express*. The Six Day Arab-Israeli war started while we were in Bulgaria, and it suddenly became impossible to make telephone or telex contact with our London offices.

We agreed that if anybody should get through we would

put over a shared story. Peter got lucky after two days of total frustration and got through to the *Sun* sports desk. He had an appalling line and was reduced to screaming 'Peter Corrigan' into the mouthpiece in a bid to make himself heard at the other end. The rest of us were gathered around him willing him to keep the precious line open. We couldn't believe it when he suddenly threw down the receiver without having dictated a word.

On the other end of the line had been Larry Coates, a veteran sub-editor with a pronounced stutter. Peter looked at us wild-eyed and said, 'I've just been told that P-P-Peter C-C-Corrigan is in B-B-Bulgaria, and then he put the phone down and cut me off ...'

You may recall the dramatic story of how Kevin Keegan was beaten up by airport guards in Belgrade during an England tour back in the summer of 1974. There was a funny side to what was a personal nightmare for Kevin. Bernard Joy, late and much respected football correspondent for the London *Evening Standard*, witnessed it all and thought he had the scoop of the season. There were only daily newspapermen on the spot with Bernard at the airport where three armed policemen laid into Keegan as if he was a drug runner. He and his Liverpool team-mate Alec Lindsay had been skylarking by the luggage conveyor belt, and the guards had reacted by frog-marching Keegan off to a side-room and beating him up as they forced him to kneel in front of them.

The incident happened right in front of a disbelieving Bernard Joy and provincial newspapers reporter Bob Harris (later Sports Editor of the *Daily* and *Sunday Mirror*). While Bob alerted tour manager Joe Mercer to what had happened, Bernard dashed to the nearest telephone. As it was early afternoon, he knew he had time to catch the late editions of the *Standard*. He dashed to a telephone and booked a call, and while he was waiting for his connection, he got first-person quotes from Mercer and even from

Keegan, talking through swollen lips and nursing a black eye and cuts.

When his call came through, the London switchboard operator on the *Standard* said in a pleasant tone: 'Good afternoon, Mr Joy. What's the weather like? It's a beautiful day here.'

Bernard snapped, 'I've got no time to discuss the weather. Put me over to the copy-takers quickly. I've got a major story.'

There was silence on the other end of the line. Then the operator said, 'But, Mr Joy, don't you realise it's Sunday. There's no paper today.'

Desmond Hackett, the legendary 'Brown Bowler' man of Fleet Street now gracing the great press box in the sky, told me he was once telephoning a story back to the *Daily Express* from South America, and because of the time difference was making the call at breakfast-time from his hotel bed. 'It was a diabolical line,' said Des, 'and to try and make myself heard I burrowed under the bedclothes with the receiver in my hand. When I finally surfaced I found the maid had been, and by the side of my bed she had left *two* cups of coffee. The mind boggles at what she must have thought I was doing under the sheets!'

Des was The Great Entertainer of Fleet Street sports columnists, who – tongue in cheek – first coined the phrase, 'Don't let facts spoil a good story'. He used to make the most outrageous predictions to force readers to sit up and take notice. Des once wrote that if Chelsea reached the FA Cup Final he would walk barefoot to Wembley. Chelsea duly battled through to the Final against Spurs in 1967.

As Des – never one to duck his duty (particularly when he knew its circulation value) – started on his barefoot walk, he was accompanied by manager Tommy Docherty and half a dozen Chelsea first-team players, who were ribbing him in good-humoured style.

A rubbish truck came slowly by and Des, without breaking step, said to the Chelsea players, 'Here you are, chaps, your coach has arrived to take you to Wembley.'

Tommy Doc, not exactly slow with the quips, applauded. 'That's Des,' he said, 'the king of the instant one-liners.'

What Des did not know is that one of the Chelsea players had put his shoes on to the rubbish truck. Happy days.

Peter Batt, a poet of a writer and one of Fleet Street's greatest characters, was a fine news reporter before switching to the sports scene. We were on the *Daily Herald* together in the early 1960s when he was ordered to hustle out to France on the first available flight to follow up a news story of a plane crash in the Pyrenees.

Peter in those days had a liking for a glass or three of 'the old sherbet' – his Cockney description for booze, the demon that he has conquered in recent years. By the time he had reached France, Peter was flying higher than the plane. He managed to persuade a taxi-driver to take him from the airport to within half a mile of the snow-hampered scene of the crash. Peter then had to walk – or, more accurately, stagger – the rest of the way. He was ill-prepared for the sudden cold, and in his legless state he tripped over a small boulder and lay face down in the snow.

A team of nuns, returning from the crash site, found him and took him to a nearby nunnery for treatment to a gashed leg. Rumour flashed back to other reporters covering the crash that a survivor had been found. They dashed to the nunnery to find Battman tucked up in bed with a warming glass of brandy in his hand. 'Cheers, chaps,' was their greeting.

If it's possible, Geoffrey Green was an even more astonishing character than Peter Batt in the days when Fleet Street bred people who were larger than life (and twice as handsome). They were total opposites: Peter, an aitch-dropping, effusive, street-wise Cockney; Geoffrey, a Corinthian-spirited, university-educated gentleman who was for many years the highly respected Association Football correspondent of *The Times* and an entertaining contributor to *Sports Report* on BBC Radio. Yet these two men (Geoffrey, alas, is no longer with us) from contrasting worlds had a central meeting point in that both were masters of the art of finding words to describe sporting events.

An idea of Geoffrey's extrovert personality can be gleaned from the fact that when a leg injury necessitated the use of a crutch he attended an England international match at Wembley with a stuffed parrot on his shoulder! Another time, my then partner Peter Lorenzo and I organised a testimonial dinner for Sir Alf Ramsey at London's Café Royal. Geoffrey, one of the finest after-dinner speakers of his or any other generation, followed the then Prime Minister Harold Wilson as speaker. He brought the house down by suggesting that, as Sir Alf was out of work, he should consider joining him in a street busking team. Geoffrey then produced a mouth organ and proceeded to play 'Moon River'. It was difficult to gauge who was more surprised or more amused, Sir Alf or the Prime Minister.

I spent many enjoyable hours in Geoffrey's company, and one story that stands out in my memory is of when, during an England tour match in Poland, he and Laurie Pignon (then on the *Daily Sketch*) were arrested for causing a disturbance in the city centre of Katowice. This was in the pre-Solidarity days, and Geoffrey was making a public speech about the values of a free society. Laurie, the absolute epitome of the 'terribly English' gentleman, who had been given a rough time as a prisoner-of-war in Poland, was seconding Geoffrey's argument.

Two guards, in ankle-length fur-lined coats, appeared from out of nowhere and marched Geoffrey and Laurie away. A few hours later, with their worried press colleagues on the point of calling in the British ambassador, they reappeared wearing broad, drunken grins and, would you believe, a fur-lined, ankle-length guardsman's coat each!

Geoffrey continued to wear his coveted coat in the press boxes of the world right up until his retirement as the man from *The Times*. I don't think lovable Laurie Pignon would have considered wearing his coat in the Wimbledon press box in his role as the distinguished lawn-tennis correspondent for the *Daily Mail*.

I was sitting alongside Geoffrey at The Dell, reporting on a Southampton match that boiled over into violence. Geoffrey, who did not think his day had started until he had polished off half a bottle of spirits, seemed more eccentric than usual when he picked up the telephone and started dictating his match report to *The Times* copytaker. 'Ding Dong Bell,' chanted Geoffrey into the receiver, 'Trouble at The Dell ...' I wondered what the sub-editor would make of that rubbish as I switched my concentration to my own description of the match. The next day I read Geoffrey's report in *The Times*. His opening line was intact and his version of events was not only poetic but captured completely what had gone on at The Dell. It put my piece in the *Express* in the shade.

Geoffrey had a habit of using song-lines when he talked, and he always greeted people with phrases like 'Younger than springtime ...' or 'Over the rainbow, baby ... ' When Bobby Moore arrived at Mexico Airport after his arrest in Bogota on a trumped-up jewel theft charge, I stood alongside Geoffrey in the throng of pressmen waiting on the Tarmac at the bottom of the plane disembarkment steps. As Bobby stood on the top step, illuminated by scores of flashing camera light bulbs, he looked down and spotted Geoffrey. He punched a fist into the air and shouted, 'Over the rainbow, baby!'

Foreign reporters, anxious to record Bobby's first words on his return to freedom, scratched their heads as they tried to decipher just what the England captain had said.

Ah, Bobby Moore ... Geoffrey Green ... Desmond Hackett. They don't make them like that any more. They were giants among men and gave so much to *This Sporting Laugh*.